Acts 29

Writing the Next Chapter

Rev. Scott Hoffman

PublishAmerica
Baltimore

© 2009 by Rev. Scott Hoffman.
All rights reserved. No part of this book may be reproduced, stored in a retrieval system or transmitted in any form or by any means without the prior written permission of the publishers, except by a reviewer who may quote brief passages in a review to be printed in a newspaper, magazine or journal.

First printing

PublishAmerica has allowed this work to remain exactly as the author intended, verbatim, without editorial input.

Scripture quotations taken from:

The HOLY BIBLE, NEW INTERNATIONAL VERSION®
© 1973, 1978, 1984 by International Bible Society.
Used by permission of Zondervan. All rights reserved.

The Message/Remix: The Bible in Contemporary Language®
© 2003, 2006 by Eugene H. Peterson.
Used by permission of Multnomah Publishers, Inc.
All rights reserved.

ISBN: 1-60836-164-0
PUBLISHED BY PUBLISHAMERICA, LLLP
www.publishamerica.com
Baltimore

Printed in the United States of America

Dedication

This book is dedicated to my incredible wife Nancy for all of your love and support and to my son Kevin, with whom I am well pleased.

But most importantly, this book is dedicated to the glory of God who through His amazing love for us sent His Son Jesus Christ to die for our sins. The least we can do in return is to become the believers He desires us to be.

This book is also dedicated to my brothers and sisters at the First Congregational Church of Chester who walked with us through these experiences and have loved us through it all.

Introduction

There have only been a few times in my life when I was absolutely certain that God was clearly calling me to do something very specifically. The first time I remember hearing His voice so clearly was in the summer of 1990. I was enjoying a respite from my work, in our new found haven in Ocean Grove. My wife and I were attending an evening session with Dan Betzer, an incredible preacher from Florida who was leading a two night preaching series in Ocean Grove. I remember sitting about half way back in the Tabernacle, listening to a wonderful message, when Rev. Betzer stopped in the middle of his message and said that God has whispered to him clearly that there was someone in the audience who was supposed to leave what they were doing and enter into full-time ministry. I knew with absolute certainty that He was talking to me. I had no interest in full-time ministry, loved my business, and was enjoying a wave of overwhelming success, but my first instinct was not one of denial, but rather one of, "why me?" The word from God was that clear. Less than two years later I was in full-time ministry. Because it was Him calling, I was able to joyfully take a pay cut from $200,000 to $24,000! Because it was Him calling, I was able to stop running my own business and traveling all around the world and, instead, become the Pastor of a dysfunctional church with 30 members that was dying a slow painful death. The initial call was a easier to answer than the sustained call of the day to day work in the ministry. After a little more than six months, we had grown the church from its 30 members to 24 members, and there wasn't a day in that first six months that I didn't ask God what in the world He was doing! But He knew and I knew that He knew and that, in the end, was sufficient. Nancy & I pastored that same church for the next 16 years and the joy of that work was unlike anything I could ever have imagined. Scores of people came to the Lord, disciples grew and prospered, missions work was started at home and around the world, people were healed, marriages repaired and strengthened, and the Gospel went out from that little church every single day! God knew what He was doing.

The next time I heard that voice so clearly was in the summer of 2001. Again, in that same Tabernacle in Ocean Grove, again on vacation and enjoying some down time from our ministry work. While in prayer during a Bible Hour session, God spoke so clearly to me that I was to donate one of my kidneys to the grandson of some friends of ours who were beginning to become desperate about his weakening condition. After sharing that incredible news with Nancy, we prayed some more and agreed that we both believed God was speaking that word to us. After an incredible series of tests, it was determined that I was a 5 of 6, or nearly perfect match for Scott's kidney and the peace that passes all understanding filled our hearts and we knew it was His call. The proof of that call came a little more than six months after the transplant when Scott grew sick from an unrelated illness and could not beat it and went home to be with the Lord. The peace that his mom displayed the night he died and the peace we all felt was so overwhelming that we knew that God had a plan all along and we trusted Him.

The most recent encounter of that magnitude with the specific instruction from the Lord was His call to Nancy & I to embark on our newest adventure as the senior staff people at our beloved Ocean Grove Camp Meeting. Leaving our church in Chester was one of the hardest things that I had ever done, we loved that place, loved those people, had roots back to 1699 in that area, and yet, God was so clear. To date, we cannot tell you how His plan is going to unfold, but we have His peace as we once again follow His lead in strange and unfamiliar landscape, in ways that don't make too much sense to the human mind and senses, but in ways only He can imagine.

I tell these stories by way of a brief introduction to our life and ministry, but also to tell you that completing this writing project is another of those strong, specific instructions from the One who knows more than I about why it is important. So, at His instruction and attempting to capture His word, here we go.

In writing this book I have gone through many different metamorphoses, and as a result, so has the focus of the project. What began as a Bible Study for pastors and church leaders, to use with their members to enhance the quality and effectiveness of their churches; has evolved into a word for all believers in these uncertain last days in which we live.

As I have read and studied Scripture over the last 30 years I have been continually drawn to the Word that God has for His church in the Book of Acts and in His Revelation to the church in the last book of the Bible. The Book of Acts is the history of His church from the very beginning at Pentecost to the death of the apostle Paul and the advancement of the church through the end of the first century. The Book of Acts is designed to show us what God had in mind for His church at its very outset, from the ascension of Christ into Heaven to the expansion of the Body of Christ throughout the known world. God has left us an instruction book for how the church is to function in the world until Christ returns for us. Luke, the physician and true companion of Paul, writes this continuation of his gospel record "*so that you may know the truth concerning the things about which you have been instructed.*" The Gospel according to Luke and the Book of the Acts of the Apostles were written as an instruction book for believers left in the world until He returns.

The Book of Revelation, as authored by the beloved apostle John, was written likewise to the Church to "*show His servants what must soon take place.*" The first three chapters of Revelation are addressed directly to the church and provide a series of instructions, warnings, commendations, and condemnations that serve as a significant guide for living for Christ to the church "*who has ears to hear.*" The first chapter of Revelation outlines the nature of the message Christ is offering to His church and the second and third chapter are specific words directly from the Lord to His universal church.

Like so many, I have read these words from Acts and Revelation over and over again for years and have always seen them as specific words and instruction to His church. By affirming my understanding that these words are addressed to the church, I was able to somehow minimize their critical importance to me personally. Surely, I accepted their validity as they spoke to the church and I employed the carefully handed down directions in my role as a pastor and teacher of the word, but there was always a thin veil between the author and the recipient. That veil was the result of reading the words of instruction as someone applying to some "third-party," a nebulous concept of a thing we call "the church." And even though I know better, I always talked about "the church" as if it were an entity of its own, an organization, a structure, something that had life and breath all by itself. I always thought about "the church" as something that could be talked about apart from the individuals who make up the church. And, as pastors are forever telling their congregations: the church is not the building; the church is not the denomination; the church is not the entity that was incorporated in 1740 or 1980 or whenever the place where you worship began.

I have come to the recent understanding that the church is not even "the people" who make it up! The church is actually, you! Whenever the Scripture speaks of "the church," we should never think of it in terms of the manifestation of His Body that meets in your town or even the collection of people who have called Him Lord since the first century. When the Scripture speaks a word of warning or instruction or commendation to "the church," it is actually God speaking directly to you. The instruction is meant for you. The warning is meant for you. The commendation is meant for you. The condemnation is meant for you. The church is you. I would challenge you to go back to the Book of Acts or the Revelation to John and re-read those books thinking of the "church" as "you." It is far more difficult to gloss over the word from Jesus that says "*He spits you out of His mouth*" when the "you" is not some nebulous church at Laodicea, but rather, the "you" is you!

When I started the work on this book, it was designed for "the church." It was designed to help "the church" respond to God's call to be His church in the 21st century. The framework for this study was to look carefully at what God is saying to His church in the letters that He instructs John to write to the specific churches of chapters 2 and 3 of Revelation. When taken together, those seven letters represent a clear and concise instruction to the church; by way of the specific example Jesus provides for us; by way of the specific instructions He offers us; by way of the specific commendations He offers for actions that are consistent with His call on the church; and, by way of the specific condemnations He makes for the actions that are significantly inconsistent with His desire for the Church. When taken together, these seven letters provide a framework for the church of Jesus Christ still today. More to the point, when taken together, these seven letters provide a very specific framework for YOU, as a the "church" of Jesus Christ for attitude and action in your life right now!

When coupled with the Book of Acts, the letters from Revelation are as clear a roadmap as we have for what God had in mind for His church and its role in the world for the kingdom. The 28 chapters of Book of Acts combine to provide the best outline that we have for what we are to be doing in and through Him in our lives today. The 28 chapters of Acts are a living history of the foundations of the church and were never intended to be anything short of an instruction manual for the church in all generations. The church is a living organism, always growing, always changing, always finding ways to re-produce itself to insure its survival.

Since the church is an ever-growing entity, the initial concept for this work was to provide a simple seven-part instruction book for the church in its next chapter, hence the title, the Acts 29 Church. This instruction book was not to reveal anything new, but rather to confirm the truths already made known to us through the inspiration of the Holy Spirit in lives of Luke and John 2000 years ago. The framework for this project was to first examine those seven letters to the church revealed to John and passed on to us. From those seven letters would emerge a rather comprehensive catalog of "dos and don'ts" for the church. This catalog, coupled with the detailed information that Dr. Luke provides for us about life in the first century church, would produce much of what we would need to help write the next chapter, Acts 29.

Given my new found understanding of the simple fact that "the church" is me and you, the real work of this project is to produce that outline for what it takes to be an Acts 29 person. Applying all that we learn from Jesus' letters to His church and all that we learn from the first folks that gathered in His name after He returned to Heaven, we can be Acts 29 kind of people...we can be His faithful followers and His devoted disciples in the 21st century.

As I sat down to write this introduction, I had just returned home from a Pastor's Prayer Summit at which Rick Warren (of "Purpose Driven Life" fame) was the keynote speaker. He talked openly about the success of his book, but he said plainly that it contained no new information, no new revelation of truth, just what most of us already know put together in a way that would be helpful to assimilate. That is precisely what you have in front of you now, a book that has no new information, no new revelation, no startling discoveries. I do hope and pray that the Holy Spirit has inspired some of this writing such that the information is helpful to you and applicable to your lives. I also pray that, with the understanding that you are the church, you will feel a greater sense of ownership and responsibility for "having ears that hear what the Spirit is saying to the church."

The format is simple. The first eight chapters are devoted to the first three chapters of Revelation and what God is saying to you as His church. Each chapter is designed to explore precisely what the

Scripture is saying and to apply that to our lives as 21st century followers. These eight chapters are designed for us to see, directly from the mouth of our Lord and Savior Jesus Christ, what traits and characteristics He commends and which He condemns. The next eight chapters are devoted to characteristics of an Acts 29 believer as lived out in the believers of the first century.

If we trust God and ask for His help, He will be faithful to provide all that we need to know, and to do what He expects of us. Waiting at the end of our journey here on earth, Jesus stands up from His place as seated on the throne and extends His nail-scarred hand to us with the overwhelming words, *"Welcome home! Well done good and faithful servant!"*

I pray you enjoy this particular segment of the journey and that you take seriously His word to you, His church.

ordinance.

[17]When I saw him, I fell at his feet as though dead. Then he placed his right hand on me and said: "Do not be afraid. I am the First and the Last. [18]I am the Living One; I was dead, and behold I am alive for ever and ever! And I hold the keys of death and Hades.

[19]"Write, therefore, what you have seen, what is now and what will take place later. [20]The mystery of the seven stars that you saw in my right hand and of the seven golden lampstands is this: The seven stars are the angels of the seven churches, and the seven lampstands are the seven churches.

it a...

Greetings and Doxology

[4]John, To the seven churches in the province of Asia:

Grace and peace to you from him who is, and who was, and who is to come, and from the seven spirits before his throne, [5]and from Jesus Christ, who is the faithful witness, the firstborn from the dead, and the ruler of the kings of the earth.

To him who loves us and has freed us from our sins by his blood, [6]and has made us to be a kingdom and priests to serve his God and Father—to him be glory and power for ever and ever! Amen. [7]Look he is coming with the clouds, and every eye will see him, even thos who pierced him; and all the peoples of the earth will mourn becau of him. So shall it be! Amen.

Chapter 1
"Blessed Because You Read"

What God Says to You as His Church

Revelation 1: 1-20

Prologue

The revelation of Jesus Christ, which God gave him to show his servants what must soon take place. He made it known by sending his angel to his servant John, [2]who testifies to everything he saw—that is, the word of God and the testimony of Jesus Christ. [3]Blessed is the one who reads the words of this prophecy, and blessed are those who hear it and take to heart what is written in it, because the time is near

[8]"I am the Alpha and the Omega," says the Lord God, "who is, and who was, and who is to come, the Almighty."

One Like a Son of Man

[9]I, John, your brother and companion in the suffering and kingdom and patient endurance that are ours in Jesus, was on the island of Patmos because of the word of God and the testimony of Jesus. [10]On the Lord's Day I was in the Spirit, and I heard behind me a loud voice like a trumpet, [11]which said: "Write on a scroll what you see and send it to the seven churches: to Ephesus, Smyrna, Pergamum, Thyatira, Sardis, Philadelphia and Laodicea."

[12]I turned around to see the voice that was speaking to me. And when I turned I saw seven golden lampstands, [13]and among the lampstands was someone "like a son of man," dressed in a robe reaching down to his feet and with a golden sash around his chest. [14]His head and hair were white like wool, as white as snow, and his eyes were like blazing fire. [15]His feet were like bronze glowing in a furnace, and his voice was like the sound of rushing waters. [16]In his right hand he held seven stars, and out of his mouth came a sharp double-edged sword. His face was like the sun shining in all its brilli...

I. Introduction

The intent of these eight chapters, which I have entitled, "What God Says To You as His Church," is to take an overview of the first three chapters of the book of Revelation. I would like us to look specifically at the letters Jesus instructed John to write to the churches, and, specifically, to us as His children.

As you read this first chapter of Revelation, you discover a very distinct chain of the revelations themselves. First God gave them to Jesus, then Jesus gave them to an angel, a messenger from heaven given the duty of carrying these messages, the angel gave them to John, and then John wrote them down for us to have 2000 years later! In these first 3 chapters, we see messages to real live churches. In this chapter, I would like to lay a foundation in the form of introduction before we study the churches.

Revelation is a book that mostly speaks of things that are yet to occur. Revelation is apocalyptic literature, which talks of events that have yet to take place, and speaks of them in the form of images and symbols. In Revelation, John does precisely what he is told to do, he writes down everything that he sees and hears. It was not John's job to interpret what he sees or to discuss the reality of what lies behind the images that he sees. It was his job to merely describe for us all that he has been blessed to witness. The bottom line of all of Revelation is this: Those who believe in Jesus Christ will live in the presence of God forever, those who do not will be forced to endure the horrible fate of eternal separation from God and all that this entails.

Prophecies have been fulfilled before, and in God's time, all will be fulfilled. The end of the times of this earth, as we know it, is closer than the world believes and there must be a new urgency in the church. The word "Revelation" comes from the Greek word from which we get our word "Apocalypse." It means the disclosure or unveiling of the truth. Even though we are going to cover the first three chapters, we must understand that this entire book is an unveiling of the judgment that will come. It is unalterable, unstoppable, unchangeable, and undeniable! To say you do not believe it does not change the fact tha' Jesus will come for His church, send tribulation to the world, returr bodily, and rule and reign forevermore. This is not an exhaustive study but hopefully a practical one.

II. The Blessings of This Word

First of all, this is not the Revelation of John, it is the Revelation o Jesus Christ as stated in verse 1. It is the Revelation of the Word tha was "made flesh and dwelt among us." The delivery agent was John

As a side note, if we study the Gospels, we find that the best frienc of Jesus while on earth was the Apostle John. Faithfulness alway⋅ brings trust. God chose to give the responsibility to pen this book tc John, in my opinion, because John was faithful. John could be trusted. so when God wanted these truths written, He dictated them to thi⋅ elderly apostle.

In Revelation, chapter one, we must notice the blessings of th⋅ Book. In verse 3, we find that there is an individual blessing for tho⋅⋅ that will read the book. It is a blessing on the one who proclaims th⋅ truth of what is revealed in its pages. It is also true that a blessing would be on the reader as well. It would do us good to note that, unlike when it was first written, today it is available for all to read for themselves.

Paul instructed Timothy to be faithful to read in 1 Timothy 4:13, that says, *"Until I come, devote yourself to the public reading of Scripture, to preaching and to teaching."* In addition, there is a blessing for those who hear. This does not mean that they merely had the sounds of the book pass through their auditory system, but that they have open ears and understand. As we will see, to all seven churches, it is said: *"He who has an ear, let him hear what the Spirit says to the churches."* Eight other times we see Jesus using the same words. God wants us to listen. How many times do we hear the words but never absorb the message? The Word of God, so many times, is clear in its instruction, that we must admit that listening is a problem for mankind. Just a few of the verses include:

> • Proverbs 19:20 *"Listen to advice and accept instruction, and in the end you will be wise!"*
> • Proverbs 15:31 *"He who listens to a life-giving rebuke will be at home among the wise."*
> • Ecclesiastes 5:1 *"Guard your steps when you go to the house of God. Go near to listen rather than to offer the sacrifice of fools, who do not know that they do wrong."*

It is necessary when we study the Word that we are careful to take the instruction that it gives. We must never be guilty of merely knowing what it says without applying it to how we live and think. Not only is there blessing for reading and hearing, but also for heeding. It says that those that "keep" the things will find blessings on their lives.

The word "keep" gives the indication that one has not only heard, but learned. After it is learned, then there is action put to the learning. That is keeping the teachings of the things found in the book, and in that, blessings are found. We must keep, learn and apply the commandments of God. This same word is used in 1 John 5:3, which says, *"This is love for God: to obey His commands."* If we are to learn the things of God, we will keep ourselves from the things of the world and focus instead on the things of God!

III. The Recipients of This Word

We have seen the blessings of this book of prophecy, now let us look at the recipients of the book. It is seen in verses 4 through 6 that the church is the target audience of what this book of prophecy contains. It was not intended for the world, though the world has used the apocalyptic messages for their own stories. It was penned for the benefit of God's people, and for His people as His church. For it is these people, the believers, who ARE His church. It is interesting to note that Jesus sent letters to seven churches. Most have agreed that the number seven is a number that represents perfection or completion. This letter was written to a complete church. Its prophecies would be fulfilled once the church was complete. We also see individual churches that are brought into the spotlight of the Scriptures, but God has His eye on us all! All but one of the churches were commended, and all but one were reprimanded. It must be noted that each church was a literal church.

Seven literal churches received letters that were dictated by Jesus and penned by the Apostle John. To our benefit, we must see that each church exhibited attributes that exist in churches today. All seven letters can be applied to each one of us as individual followers of Christ for our own benefit. We must see each church as a literal church, yet the messages are to be applied to our lives today! Elements of all still exist, even within each of our lives. At the same time, it is evident that dominant traits exist in the past and exist today. Each letter is addressed to the angel. That is the earthly leader of the church, the pastor. The word "angel" means a messenger that is sent from God. One commentator wrote that this angel of these churches was "the minister; the presiding presbyter; the bishop—in the primitive sense of the word bishop—denoting one who had the spiritual charge of a congregation." It is this leader who would expound the message to the church, and this leader who would give an account for the message being delivered. These "angels" had a great responsibility before them.

These letters were written to those who had experienced the love of God. The love of God is the very essence of the "church." How wonderful it is to recognize that God loves us. Think of Galatians 2:20 *"I have been crucified with Christ and I no longer live, but Christ lives in me. The life I live in the body, I live by faith in the Son of God, who loved me and gave Himself for me."* It is a personal love. He loved me. It is a priceless love, because Jesus, God incarnate, gave Himself for me. It is beyond our imagination and intellect to comprehend this gift. We cannot explain it, but we can accept it. Not only are the believers loved, but they have been washed. This word is one that was used to describe the process of washing blood out of a wound so that it would heal properly. Jesus has washed all of my impurities away with HIS blood.

The same word is used to describe what the Philippian jailer did for Paul and Silas. In Acts 16:33, it says, *"At that hour of the night the jailer took them and washed their wounds; then immediately he and all his family were baptized."* He washed their stripes to prevent infection. And Jesus washed me clean so that the impurity of my sin would be eternally purged. Not only are we loved and washed, but we have been elevated to a new position.

According to verse 6, we have been made to be kings and priests.

And Jesus did that for us. We are kings because our ancestry has been replaced. The bloodline of Adam has been replaced in the believer with the bloodline that gives the rights to the throne of God.

We are blood relation to Jesus by His own blood. He has made us kings.

But not only has our ancestry been replaced but our access has been changed. We are priests. A priest is one who is granted access. A priest can go directly to God. We do not have to go through the old priesthood to access the Holy of Holies, we can now approach God ourselves. Jesus has changed our access. In 1 Peter 2:5, the Bible says, *"You also, like living stones, are being built into a spiritual house to be a holy priesthood, offering spiritual sacrifices acceptable to God through Christ Jesus."* Our sacrifices are not those of rams, goats, and doves, but Spiritual sacrifices of our lives and worship.

IV. The Redeemer of This Book

We have seen the blessings of this book and the recipients of the book, but nothing would be of value without the Redeemer of the book. This is His distinction. Have you ever looked up "redeemer" in a Thesaurus? It was interesting to me that when I referenced the word in the Thesaurus, it said, *"Christ, Immanuel, Jehovah, Messiah, and*

Savior. " If a secular Thesaurus can admit it, what is wrong with the world? Our Lord has the distinction of being a faithful witness. He is the Truth, He is the source of Truth. A witness is one that can tell the truth of something. Our Faithful Witness was faithful unto death. He is supreme in death because He is supreme in His resurrection.

Others were raised from the dead, but none but Christ remained that way. Jesus is above all others because of His resurrection. He lives so that all who trust Him can live. He is also supreme because of His authority. Matthew 28:18 reveals that all power in heaven and earth is Christ's. In our text, He is called "the prince of the kings of the earth."

This shows that He is supreme in His reign. He is the Chief ruler over all authority. We also see His Deity.

In verses 8 and 11, He declares Himself as the Alpha and Omega. These are the first and last letters of the Greek alphabet. He is the first and the last and all that is in between! Colossians 1:16-17 declares, *"For by Him all things were created: things in heaven and on earth, visible and invisible, whether thrones or powers or rulers or authorities; all things were created by Him and for Him. He is before all things, and in Him all things hold together."*

He is Jehovah, the self existent God that needs no other. All things were begun by Him, and all things will end by Him. He is the Almighty, "which is, which was and which is to come."

The Revelation of Jesus Christ is a book that blesses its recipients with a message from the Almighty Redeemer. So it should be read and applied by each one of us as individuals, not simply by collections of believers nominally known as "churches."

V. Conclusion

In this first chapter we also notice an incredible urgency. Why are we blessed to read, listen and heed these writings? First of all, it is declared in verse three that *"the time is near."* The time of serving God, reaching the lost, and the time of opportunity to believe is NOW.

Romans 13:11 states, "*And do this, understanding the present time. The hour has come for you to wake up from your slumber, because our salvation is nearer now than when we first believed.*"

Every day that we live and every breath that we breathe brings us closer to the redemption of our bodies and the gathering of the church to Christ.

James 5:8 says, "*You too, be patient and stand firm, because the Lord's coming is near!*" The early church believed in the imminent return of Christ. The early church believed that the return of Christ could come at any moment. They were not expecting to go through the tribulation. I realize there are some verses that can be interpreted differently, but when we see the expectations of the early believers, it seems so simple. They were waiting, actually looking for Jesus to return.

1 Thessalonians 1:10, says, "*and to wait for His Son from heaven, whom He raised from the dead...Jesus, who rescues us from the coming wrath!*" And here's the fact: Jesus will return for His church!

Jesus is coming and everyone will be judged. And that coming could be any minute! Right this minute we are living in a day of grace.

We have been given the message of hope! Our name can be in the book! We can see God do great things and we should. We can enjoy the benefits of all that God can do in us and through us. There is nothing greater than knowing that you have the security of knowing your name is penned in the Lamb's book of Life. And there is coming a day very soon that God will remove His church, that He will remove you as a believer, and I am certain that it will be before He pours His wrath upon the world.

Are you ready for that day? We call the event the Rapture because Jesus will snatch away those that belong to Him. This is not sensationalism, this is not the stuff of movies or Left Behind fiction novels, this is Biblical truth. The saved, those who are truly a part of the body of Christ will be with Him forever! If you are a believer, then the Book of Revelation, the Apocalypse should be even greater motivation for you to tell others about Jesus! We are to rejoice and be ready. I read the story of a poor servant-boy named John that worked for a rich doctor in London, England. John's master loved the Lord Jesus and often had church meetings in the large living room of his home. At one of these meetings the doctor talked about the coming of the Lord Jesus to take to Heaven all those who believe in Him. Everyone else, he said, would be left behind. After the meeting was over, the doctor said, *"Well, John, I just want to tell you that if Jesus comes before I die, I shall no longer want the things I have now. He will take me away with Him and then you may have my house and all my money."* Such an offer took John by surprise. He could only stammer his thanks. That night he lay awake wondering why his master had offered him all that wealth. Suddenly he thought, *"Why should I want a house and furniture, a car, horses, and money after the Lord comes? How terrible it would be to be left behind, even if all my master's belongings were mine!"* Soon he could bear the thought no longer. He slipped out of bed, ran quickly down the hall to the room where his master slept and knocked on the door. *"Why, John,"* asked the doctor, *"what's the matter? What do you want?"* *"Please sir,"* answered John, *"I don't want your house after the Lord comes, or your car, or horses, or money."* *"Well, John, what do you want?"* *"Oh sir, I want to be ready when the Lord comes, to go with Him to Heaven."* Right there in the doctor's bedroom John put his trust in the Lord Jesus. Right there John was saved. Right there John was ready for the Lord's coming.

It is imperative, as we begin this work, that we recognize the importance of believing that Jesus is coming again. People are dying without Christ while the church has become apathetic. We must take these telegrams to the church to heart and return to the God that has redeemed us.

Chapter 2
"Falling in Love Again!"

What God Says to You as His Church?

Revelation 2: 1-7

To the Church in Ephesus

[1]"To the angel[a] of the church in Ephesus write: These are the words of him who holds the seven stars in his right hand and walks among the seven golden lampstands: [2]I know your deeds, your hard work and your perseverance. I know that you cannot tolerate wicked men, that you have tested those who claim to be apostles but are not, and have found them false. [3]You have persevered and have endured hardships for my name, and have not grown weary. [4]Yet I hold this against you: You have forsaken your first love. [5]Remember the height from which you have fallen! Repent and do the things you did at first. If you do not repent, I will come to you and remove your lampstand from its place. [6]But you have this in your favor: You hate the practices of the Nicolaitans, which I also hate. [7]He who has an ear, let him hear what the Spirit says to the churches. To him who overcomes, I will give the right to eat from the tree of life, which is in the paradise of God.

I. Introduction

As we consider this first church to whom Jesus dictated a letter, it would be worthwhile to spend a moment on the background of the city of Ephesus. It was a prosperous city with a strong commerce. It was a very political city, considered free by even the Romans with its own democratic government. It also was a pagan city. A temple to the goddess Diana, one of the seven architectural wonders of the world, was located in this city. It was a massive 425 feet long and 220 feet broad, about 1 ½ football fields! It contained 127 pillars that were 60 feet high. The idolatrous worshipers would worship the moon in her name. This city was one of wealth and wickedness, and yet it had a Christian church that was faithful.

For three years Paul labored there. In Acts 18-20, we find that Paul led Aquilla and Priscilla to the Lord. Apollos came and preached the baptism of John the Baptist and was corrected and began to preach Jesus. A nucleus was formed and the Gospel began to spread. Then opposition came. Demetrius the silversmith was angry that Paul's preaching had hurt his business that drew support from the worship of idols. Opposition always comes when you are doing right! But Paul kept preaching. In Acts 19:18-20, we read, *"Many of those who believed now came and openly confessed their evil deeds. A number who had practiced sorcery brought their scrolls together, and burned them publicly. When they calculated the value of the scrolls, the total came to fifty thousand drachmas. In this way, the word of the Lord spread widely and grew in power."* Paul subsequently ordained Timothy as the pastor over this city that meant so much to him. And the apostle John, toward the end of his life, after returning from exile, actually pastored in Ephesus as well. Revival broke out in the city of Ephesus.

Do any of you remember a revival in your own heart when you were actually thrilled to throw away the old because the new was so much better? That's what was happening to the people in Ephesus!

They had a fire about them. They had a fervor to live for the Lord that abounded in their lives. But somewhere on the journey, they lost the fervor! They needed to go back and be reminded of where it all began!

II. The Letter to the Church at Ephesus

This letter to the church at Ephesus begins with a commendation in verses 2-3 and in verse 6. The grace of Jesus is so evident here that even as He begins to correct His church, He begins with a gracious encouragement; oh if we could only learn from His example.

They were commended for three things needed in the church today, and remember, three things that are needed in our lives as believers as well.

First, they were commended for their deeds that were evident for all to see. Jesus said in verse 2, *"I know your deeds."* God knows our deeds and wants our future to be right. God approved of the deeds of this church. The works of which He speaks relates to how we occupy our time. The things that occupy our time either honors God, disregards Him, or dishonors Him. God should be involved in every area of our lives. Our family, jobs, ministries, and even recreation should honor the Lord.

Secondly, Jesus also knew their hard work. The word used here means intense labor that is united with trouble and toil. I read somewhere that there are three kinds of Christians in the church.

First there are "shirkers," those that have not done anything and do not plan on starting anything any time soon. Then there are the "lurkers" that hang around saying how everything ought to be done, they may get a little involved, but they never give or commit too much. There are a lot of retired Christians in the lurkers club. Then there are the "workers." This is the inner circle that knows what it means to labor. They are the most involved, faithful in all, those who will give all and never complain. Their desire to be faithful to the Lord is what drives them and keeps the church and their lives a place that honors the Lord. Jesus saw those in Ephesus who were working in His vineyard and He commended them for their labors! As a living and breathing arm of the church of Jesus Christ, which title best characterizes you?

Third, Jesus recognized their patience. The word here means

endurance, HUPOMONE, it means to "hold up under!" The church of Ephesus was a tough church. They never gave in to the temptation to throw up their hands and quit. They kept moving forward. They were persistent, faithful and refused to faint. Jesus then noted their discipline against evil in verses 2 and 6. They could not bear and would not tolerate evil in the church. The modern doctrine of tolerance would not be tolerated in the church at Ephesus!

Today the most intolerant people are those who yell for tolerance. Today it is OK to be anything but a Christian who believes what the Bible says about Jesus being the only Way!

That is precisely what happened to us in Ocean Grove when we took a stand for the sanctity of marriage and the sanctity of our worship space in the face of rising calls for the legitimacy of same sex unions. We were vilified as intolerant and bigoted for standing on the Truth of the Word. This was a battle for those who were called to be a part of it as the church of Jesus Christ, not the battle of a specific church or all the membership thereof, but a battle for the Church as embodied in those who stood firm.

The church at Ephesus would not tolerate that kind of evil. This was a church that took a stand for the things of Christ. They knew that problems exist whenever sin is tolerated. Many times people want to say, *"the preacher should do something about it."* But here it was the entire church that stood together in unity against sin. They despised loose living. This church hated the practices of the Nicolaitans, they despised these teachings because it was a dogma of wickedness. It is most likely that the Nicolaitans were a group that condoned sexual immorality and had turned Christian liberty into a license to sin. Much like many churches today that no longer preach holiness. Holy living is not legalism! The liberty of Christ has never been a license to sin. And even though there have been countless explanations as to who the Nicolatians were, the only thing we need to know is that the church at Ephesus despised the ways of these who were opposed to the things of Christ. They were opposed because their doctrine was sound.

Believing God and His doctrine was not a problem for this church. They had tried those that had come and claimed to have been apostles and found them to be liars. They identified false teachers and rejected false doctrine. The modern church and modern believers need a good dose of this. Just about anyone who comes along speaking kindly and offering solutions to today's problems is embraced by modern Christianity.

We need to be more like the church at Ephesus in this way and identify true men and women of God. However, after those kind words of acknowledgement, Jesus goes to the heart of their problem.

It was a problem of their heart. Imagine being praised by the Lord.

Imagine as they read the first part of the Letter to the church, how the church erupted into "amen!" All of the sudden the mood changes.

There is a shocking announcement, "*Yet I hold this against you!*"

How could this be? They were faithful in deed and doctrine, but their hearts were calloused. The shocking announcement was that this church had a shameful abandonment. They had left their first fervor. their first love of the Lord. They had not lost their salvation, but they had grown accustomed to it. The word here for love is the deepest and most meaningful word for love. In the book of Ephesians, a letter written by Paul to a church he loved over thirty years prior to the writing of the Revelation, there are around twenty references to love. A few of those are:

- Ephesians 1:15 "*For this reason, ever since I heard about your faith in the Lord Jesus and your love for all the saints.*"
- Ephesians 3:17 "*So that Christ may dwell in your hearts through faith. And I pray that you, being rooted and established in love, may have power...*"
- Ephesians 3:19 "*And to know this love that surpasses knowledge, that you may be filled to the measure of all the fullness of God.*"
- And Ephesians 6:23-24, Paul concludes his letter with,

"Peace to the brothers, and love with faith from God the Father and the Lord Jesus Christ. Grace to all who love our Lord Jesus Christ with an undying love. Amen"

The fact is God wants our hearts as well as our hands and heads! Imagine this scenario, a father and daughter always spent time together. All of the sudden the girl was withdrawn. The father was going to speak to her, but before he could his birthday came around.

His daughter came in with a beautiful gift. He thanked her and said, *"Dear, it was so nice of you to buy this for me"* She said, *"I didn't buy it, I made it."* The father said, *"O that is what you have been doing for the last three months."* That made the girl curious, and she asked, *"How did you know that I had been working on them for three months?"* The father answered, *"That is how long I have been missing your company."* The father was glad to have the gift, but he wanted the presence of his daughter as well.

We want to serve the Lord, and He wants us to serve Him, but He wants us to love Him first. When we serve without loving Him, the service is empty.

After the criticism, they are faced with a charge from Christ. They are told to remember. They were literally told to "call to mind constantly" the grace of God and from whence they had come. We should remind ourselves of the grace of God, where we would be had He not saved us and from whence WE have come.

III. Application

We must remember from where we have come. We also must remember TO where we have come. We are no longer dead in sins, but alive in Jesus Christ. We no longer belong to the lost, but are members of the family of God and should be delighted. We are not bound in our trespasses and sins, but our members are to be yielded to righteousness.

So what are we to do? We must remember and repent. God's children need to repent, turn from our wicked ways and run back to

God. We must confess that we have failed the Lord in not loving Him as we should. We should be broken hearted and humbled that God desires us to love Him. We are not even worthy to breathe His air, yet He wants us to love Him. When we are humbled and broken, God will draw close. Psalm 34:18 gives a great promise to the ones who are genuinely broken before God. It says, *"The LORD is close to the brokenhearted and saves those who are crushed in spirit."* The Lord gets up close when our hearts are broken. After we remember and repent, then we are to return. We must fall before the Lord and go back to the original fellowship we had when we were first saved.

We are to do the first works. This is not speaking of being saved again, rather, it is saying that we should return to living with the same fervor that we had when we first became members of the family of God. Many a young Christian has made the mistake of over zealousness, but they loved the Lord. God wants us to grow but never to let our love waver. I have been guilty of this. Sadly, we get so consumed in what is around us that we get over the joy and love of being saved. Oh that God would forgive us and help us to return to our first love. Jesus now adds the consequence of disobedience to this challenge. Chastisement will come and will come quickly. After chastisement, if the church does not repent, if we do not repent, there will be an extinguishment, the death of our ministry. Jesus will remove our lampstand, our light will go out!

IV. Conclusion

Sadly, history declares that the church at Ephesus did not listen and the Muslim religion engulfed the region and their light did go out!

Jesus kept His promise. This vibrant church of the New Testament lost their first love and was overtaken in false doctrines. The church is in great danger of this again. We are in great danger of this again! We must return to the genuine love of our God and serve Him on that basis. Not on the basis of duty or pride, but because we genuinely love Him.

In verse 7 there is a promise to those who are genuinely converted. Believers are revealed as those who over come, those who are victorious over this life through Christ. This is not a new word from Jesus, He declared on the night of the Last Supper, in John 16:33, *"I have told you these things, so that in me you may have peace. In this world you will have trouble. But take heart! I have overcome the world."* John understood the word as well for he had wrote it himself in 1 John 4:4, *"You dear children, are from God and have overcome them, because the one who is in you is greater than the one who is in the world."*

The idea of overcoming the world by the grace of God was not a new doctrine, but rather, a fact of position. Jesus has overcome the world and so will His children. Those who are genuinely saved will have the privilege of eating at the banquet table of heaven. We will be allowed to approach the tree of life and eat of its fruit. Sinners will not approach this tree, only those who have been redeemed and changed. Only those who will experience this corruption putting on incorruption, as Paul describes in his closing words of his first letter to the Corinthians. Revelation 22:14 refers to this food: *"Blessed are those who wash their robes, that they may have the right to the tree of life, and may go through the gates into the city."*

We must conclude by what we have seen that the work of the church of Ephesus was not the problem. God approved of their work.

Their problem was their level of love. I am sure that they would tell you that they loved the Lord, but God knew their hearts. Their lives had become mechanical. We must be careful that our messages, our ideas and even our questions are clear. What is it going to take for us to fall in love with Jesus again? Ephesus was much like many of our cities in America. Prosperous, no major problems and God's people were rocked to sleep by the devil. Just like the words of the Casting Crowns song captures: *"We've been lulled to sleep by philosophies that save the trees and kill the children."* Everyone should minister, everyone should serve. But the devil does not care if you serve, as long as you do not love the Lord while you're doing it! What if we had a Love Meter? On that meter it would show our level of fervor, passion, excitement, devotion, dedication, and loyalty to God, but the greatest measurement would be our love.

What should motivate us to love Jesus? I am reminded of the first verse of "At The Cross:" "*Alas! And did my Savior bleed? And did my Sovereign die? Would He devote that sacred head For sinners such as I!*" How can I not love Him back?

There is the story of a young girl who rebelled and ran away from home. She ran to a large city that was close to home. Before long she had no way of supporting herself. Frustrated by the city and her circumstances, she entered a house of prostitution. Her mother missed the daughter greatly. She had heard somewhat of her daughter's plight, so she went to the large city and desperately sought to rescue her. She sought until her money was exhausted.

Not having her child's address, she left a photograph of herself in each house of ill fame visited. One day, the errant girl saw on a mantle in a reception room, a familiar picture. It was the likeness of her first love, her mother. She went over and took the picture of that one who had loved her and gazed at the picture. She then notices beneath the picture, two words. Those two words were not meant for any other person that came into that place, only for her. It was she who belonged to her mother. Those words were, "come home." And the girl did, she ran home to the first one she ever loved!

We may run from God, but He desires us to come home and love him once again. The most miserable person on the face of this world is not the sinner, but the believer that is no longer in love with the Lord. Have you left your first love? He wants you back!!

Chapter 3
"The Cowardly Lion's Plea...Courage!"

What God Says to You as His Church

Revelation 2: 8-11

To the Church in Smyrna
[8]"To the angel of the church in Smyrna write:
These are the words of him who is the First and the Last, who died and came to life again. [9]I know your afflictions and your poverty—yet you are rich! I know the slander of those who say they are Jews and are not, but are a synagogue of Satan. [10]Do not be afraid of what you are about to suffer. I tell you, the devil will put some of you in prison to test you, and you will suffer persecution for ten days. Be faithful, even to the point of death, and I will give you the crown of life. [11]He who has an ear, let him hear what the Spirit says to the churches. He who overcomes will not be hurt at all by the second death."

I. Introduction
We should not forget that as we continue our look at the first 3 chapters of Revelation, we can apply the letters to these churches three ways. First that these are literal churches. The beauty of our Bible is that we can prove that the places named actually exist, or at least existed at the time John wrote these letters. Second, it can be seen from where we stand today that each church can represent a portion of the church age throughout its history. Finally, it also is

evident that each one shows elements that are present in churches today, more specifically, that they can be applied to each and every single one of us as "the Church" of Jesus Christ. It is my contention that none of these interpretations are mutually exclusive, but what matters most to us, as His followers, as His disciples, as His children wishing to be obedient to His call on our lives right now, is that these letters are hand written from the throne of God Himself, directly to you and me!

With all of that being said, let's take a closer look at this second letter in this chapter.

Smyrna was a wealthy city second only to Ephesus among the seven churches on this list. It was located about 35 miles north of Ephesus. Its main product was myrrh, a perfume taken from tree bark, used in embalming, most notably recognized as one of the three gifts the Magi brought to Jesus. Its name means bitter, which is a good name for what they faced. Located on a gulf of the Aegean, it was one of the great cities of Asia, a seat of emperor worship with a large temple to Tiberius. Some think the present angel or pastor of this church, was Polycarp, the disciple of John. We'll come back to him in a little while. The history of the planting of this church is unknown, but it was possibly started under Paul's supervision. During the second century, the church was prominent, and from the moment of its founding, it has never ceased to exist. It is the only church of the seven that has been in continual operation since the first century.

Paul possibly helped start this church on his third missionary journey as seen in Acts 19.

II. A Reminder of the Author

As we approach this letter to the church at Smyrna, we are convinced of the Originator, the true Author. In verse 8, it is declared that this message is coming from the One that is the First and the Last. Call Him the Champion, Winner, Victor, Master, or any other name you might call one who cannot be defeated, but the best name for Him is God. He is the first to exist, He is ever existing and He is not ever going away. If eternity had a beginning and ending, Jesus would dwell outside its boundaries. One of my seminary professors was fond of saying, *"There never was a time that Jesus wasn't!"* I like that expression. This letter was dictated directly from God Himself.

The same title is used in Isaiah 44:6, that says, *"This is what the Lord says, Israel's King and Redeemer the LORD almighty; I am the first, and I am the last; apart from me there is no God."*

Another revelation of the Author is that He is the One who died and is Alive. The resurrection proves it all. Revelation 1:18 declares, *"I am the Living One; I was dead, and behold I am alive for ever and ever! And I hold the keys of death and Hades!"* It is His deity that is proven by the resurrection. All power is His as the Conqueror of death. He is Lord of all and is sending a message to His church.

Sadly, the churches then, just as today, do not listen well, even though there is a clear mandate directly from the throne of God.

This letter is coming from Jesus!

III. The Letter

The letter opens with our reminder of its true authorship, and the very next statement is one that could be seen in a mixed light, yet one that should make us aware of a simple fact. God knows our works, whether they be good or bad. Adversity was rampant for this church. Jesus declared to them that in the midst of what they were facing, He knew their works. He knew if they were good or bad, real or fake, faithful or half-hearted. He knew if it was moral or immoral, He knew their works. In 2 Timothy 2:19, a simple statement of fact declares to God's church what Jesus knows and expects. It says, *"Nevertheless God's solid foundation stands firm, sealed with this inscription: 'The Lord knows those who are His', and, 'Everyone who confesses the name of the Lord must turn away from wickedness.'"* God knows who is His and those who are His are sealed forever. He is aware of all of our works, and if we belong to Him, we are to turn away from wickedness. This is an imperative, this is not a suggestion. Many who call themselves Christians are guilty of not heeding this command. It means that we are to shun, to flee from, to stand off from, to remove yourself from anything that violates God's Word and His sense of justice or any act of unrighteousness. Jesus was aware of all their works, good and bad.

Another thing of which He was aware was that trials and tribulations were abounding for these people. No matter what we face, we must remember that God knows where we are and what we are facing. As I wrote this message, I am painfully aware of the fact that many of us are facing some extraordinarily painful experiences in our lives. In fact, He told us very plainly that *"in this world you will have trouble, but,"'* He said, *"take heart, for I have overcome the world!"* One of the extraordinary things about the Lord that we serve is that not only is He aware of the pain and trials we face, but we can know that He understands because He faced the same things that we face, only worse! Why do you think that Jesus wept at the tomb of Lazarus? It was not that He could not do anything, but rather, He knew the troubled hearts, the pain, and, most importantly, He knew the effects of our sin. No matter what we face, Jesus knows and loves us. The great security passage, in Romans 8, says in verses 35-39, *"Who shall separate us from the love of Christ? Shall trouble or hardship or persecution or famine or nakedness, or danger or sword? As it is written, For your sake we face death all the day long; we are considered as sheep to be slaughtered. No, in all these things we are more than conquerors through him who loved us. For I am convinced, that neither death nor life, neither angels nor demons, neither the present nor things the future, nor any powers, neither height nor depth, nor anything else in all creation will be able to separate us from the love of God, that is in Christ Jesus our Lord."*

The truth is that the storms of this life have come, will come, and are coming. This is not such a great comfort in the midst of trials, but even so it is the truth, nothing, absolutely nothing, can separate me from the love of God. With His love comes awareness, and with that awareness I have the assurance of His presence in my life! Jesus also notes their poverty. This is not the poverty of the lost, rather these people had lost all for the sake of Christ. This loss of substance is Christ-like. This is the loss that Paul talks about in 2 Corinthians relative to the fact that Jesus was rich and yet for our sakes became poor. Their poverty also was Christ-honoring. These are people who did not regard earthly possessions more highly than their position in Christ. Yes, they had faced and were living in poverty, but they had a treasure that most would never see. The wealth was that they were poor on earth, but rich in heaven. That is real wealth.

They were rich in salvation. Think about this wealth and what it provides. In John 11:26, before Lazarus was raised from the dead, Jesus declared to Martha, *"I am the resurrection and the life. He who believes in me will live, even though he dies; and whoever lives and believes in me will never die, Do you believe this?"* To know that we will live in Christ forever is a wealth beyond anything this world can offer. They also were rich in heavenly places. These pilgrims had treasures laid up in heaven. There is nothing wrong with earthly wealth unless it controls you. But earthly wealth must never come before our relationship with God. It does not matter if it is a career or hobby, nothing should ever supercede our relationship, stewardship, or fellowship with Jesus Christ. We are to give God what is rightfully His and be willing to give all to and for Him. That is how this church was existing as declared by Jesus Himself. How cool would that be to be said of us? They were earthly poor, but they were in reality, rich. Though poverty was an earthly attribute, the reality was their wealth as declared by Christ.

They not only faced adversity, but they had to deal with the anxieties of their situation. They had to face the attack of "legalists."

There is much misunderstanding of this word today. Some want to call strong standards legalism. Sadly, most who want to cry legalism are only doing so because they want to throw some standard aside.

Realistically, there are some who have taken standards to a level that is ridiculous, but we should never think that we can abuse our liberty in Christ. Legalism is by definition those who want to mix the law with grace. This was a common problem in the early church. Many tried to hold on to traditions and rudiments of the time before Christ and mix it with the complete work of our Lord. We need not add any work to the work of Christ for our salvation. This does not mean we can do as we please. We will live for Christ because we are saved, not in order to be saved.

The other extreme already had been condemned by Christ in dealing with Ephesus. The Nicolaitians abused their liberties to sin.

In the church at Smyrna, there were those who wanted to bind the church by the sacraments and traditions of the Law, which Christ had fulfilled and nailed to His cross! Colossians 2:8 deals with this, *"See to it that no one takes you captive through hollow and deceptive philosophy, which depends on human tradition and the basic principles of this world rather than on Christ."* The law shows us that we need a Savior, we are sinners, but His judgment is no longer against those that are redeemed by the blood of Jesus. Colossians 2:13-14 says, *"When you were dead in your sins and in the uncircumcision of your sinful nature, God made you alive with Christ.*

He forgave us all our sins, having canceled the written code, with its regulations, that was against us and that stood opposed to us; He took it away, nailing it to the cross!" What is even worse is that this desire to return to the written laws and codes was coming from religious people who weren't true believers! Jesus tells us plainly in this letter that these people were not of a synagogue of God, were not in the family of God, but were actually "a synagogue of Satan."

In verse 10 of our text we see an attack of fear. The emotion of fear is a normal reaction of our flesh. If we struggle, it is not wondering if God can do anything or if He is sufficient. Most of the time what we are fearful of is really just the circumstances of our lives or maybe even the unknown. Advice is more easily received when we are not in the midst of trouble, but when trouble comes we must return to God's Word and remember what we have been instructed to do. In the case of these that were being martyred, Jesus had taught in Matthew 10:19, *"But when they arrest you, do not worry about what to say or how to say it. At that time you will be given what to say..."* God is in control.

In the trials of daily life, fear must be rejected by believing the principle taught in Matthew 6, that says, *"Therefore I tell you, do not worry about your life, what you will eat or drink; about about your body, what you will wear. For the pagans run after all these things, and your heavenly Father knows that you need them. But seek first His kingdom and His righteousness, and all these things will be given to you as well."* The preeminence of Christ answers the fears of supply. And though it is hard, we are commanded in Philippians 4:6 to *"Do not be anxious about anything, but in every thing by prayer and petition with thanksgiving let your requests be made known unto God."*

I must confess this is not always easy for any of us, it wasn't easy for the early church either, but it was possible or Christ would not have told them not to fear. If Jesus tells us to do it, He will enable us to do it.

Verse 10 also reveals that afflictions are coming. A spiritual attack of great proportion was indeed coming. The devil was going to attack! We must never give into the devil, never offer him any ground whatsoever, but we must always admit and confess that we face a spiritual battle everyday. How many times have our hearts been broken because someone has given into an attack. An interesting passage is found in the tenth chapter of Daniel. Daniel had been praying for three weeks, and no immediate answer came. Finally an angel came and picked Daniel up off the floor. In verses 12 and 13, Daniel says that the angel said to him, *"Do not be afraid, Daniel. Since the first day that you set your mind to gain understanding and to humble yourself before your God, your words were heard, and I have come in response to them.*" There was spiritual warfare of extreme proportions in Daniel's life and yet, when he set his mind on the Lord, He was there!

How much more do we need to pray and to seek the face of God? He will fight for us. Paul faced similar battles, as he explained in Ephesians 6:12 that our battle is not of this world, "*For we wrestle not against flesh and blood, but against principalities, against powers, against the rulers of the darkness of this world, against spiritual wickedness in high places.*" We must be prepared for spiritual battle. Just because we deny a spiritual battle does not remove it or make it non-existent. We must fight and protect ourselves with the armor of God as we face spiritual attack

The church at Smyrna also was facing some coming physical attacks. Prison and even worse fates were facing them. Historically we read that their pastor, Polycarp was martyred when he would not recant his Christian faith and he was burned at the stake. It has been placed around A.D. 168, eighty-six years after his conversion. I read that he said: "*Fourscore and six years have I served the Lord, and He has never wronged me: How then can I blaspheme my King and Savior.*" This persecution was beyond anything that modern American Christians have imagined. Christians were crucified, burned as street lights, pierced with multiple wounds, fed to the lions, and boiled in hot oil. All of these things faced the church of that day. Jesus did give comfort that the persecutions would not be forever.

He says that their tribulation would be ten days. Some believe it has to do with the ten Roman rulers from 160 to 313 AD who persecuted the church beginning with Nero and ending with Diocletian. Others believe it had to do with the last ruler, Diocletian who reigned for 10 years. Either way, God told them it would come, but it would end.

Our troubles may not pass how and when we desire, but they do pass.

IV. The Assurance of Jesus Christ

Along with all of the trouble that faced this church, they were given some assurances. It may not seem like a great assurance, but for the early church a confirmation from God that all is well would have been welcomed. Jesus told them that they would share His cross as they would be faithful all the way to death. We should beg God to help us be so faithful. They would also share His crown. The crown of life is one of five crowns in the Bible. This one seems to be one given to those who love and look for the return of Christ. It also is one given to those who face troubles in the Christian walk. The same crown is mentioned in James 1:12. It says, *"Blessed is the man who perseveres under trial, because he has stood the test, he will receive the crown of life that God has promised to those who love him."*

When martyr John Huss, one of the predecessors of Martin Luther in the reform movement, was to be burned, a paper crown with painted devils was put on him. He declared, *"My Lord Jesus Christ, for my sake, wore a crown of thorns: why should I not wear, for His sake, this light crown, be it ever so ignominious?"* Then the bishops said, *"Now we commit thy soul to the Devil."* *"But I,"* said Huss, lifting his eyes to heaven, *"do commit my spirit into thy hands, O Lord Jesus Christ!"* Huss, as well as these early saints in Smyrna, realized that they would only die once.

All of us participate in the first birth and the first death, but if we participate in the second birth, that is we are "born again," we will not face the second death. Physical death my take these bodies, but because of the Spiritual birth, the saved will never face the second death.

V. Conclusion

The letter to this church seems to be gloom and doom. Yes, they were being warned of the rough time that they would face. Our forefathers in the church faced torment and torture beyond our understanding, but there is a very comforting phrase in verse 9 with which we have dealt, "*I Know!*" Yes, this phrase could bring conviction with the recognition that God knows all, but, above all, it is a phrase of comfort. No matter what we face or where we may be on the journey. No matter what we do or think or say, Jesus knows. 2 Corinthians 3:5 says, "*Not that we are competent in ourselves to claim anything for ourselves, but our competence come from God!*" We must rest and rely in that sufficiency. Take the advice in Isaiah 35:4 and "*Say to those with fearful hearts, 'Be strong, do not fear; your God will come, He will come with vengeance; with divine retribution He will come to save you!*" We may face tribulation, persecution, ridicule, and even death, only God knows. Whatever we face though, He is faithful.

Years ago a woman, with her little baby, was riding in a stagecoach in western Montana. The weather was bitter cold, and, in spite of all the driver could do to protect her, he saw that the mother was becoming unconscious from the cold. He did something next that was seemingly cruel. He stopped the coach, took the baby, and wrapping it warmly, put it under the seat. He then seized the mother by the arm, dragged her out of the coach and put her upon the ground. He then did the unthinkable. In the cold weather, he drove away, leaving the mother in the road. As she saw him drive away, she ran after him, crying for her baby. Frantically she cried and ran after that coach. The driver was merely saving her life. He watched closely and maintained just the right speed. When he felt sure that the mother was warm from her exertion, he allowed her to overtake the coach and rejoin her baby. The trial had a purpose.

Only God knows what we will face and why, but our trust must be that God knows what is best. I am sure that mother did not see it was best until she was reunited with her baby and realized that the coach driver had in reality saved her live. We must live with the acknowledgement that our life belongs to Christ. One martyr said to his executioner, "*You take a life I cannot keep, and bestow a life*

41

I cannot lose; which is as if you rob me of counters, and furnish me with gold. "(– DL Moody Bishop Hugh Latimer)

We may not have to die for Him, but will we live for Him with the same passion? When we need courage we must turn back to the promises of God and realize that He knows.

Chapter 4
"The Church Where Anything Goes"

What God Says to You as His Church

Revelation 2: 12-17

To the Church in Pergamum

[12]"To the angel of the church in Pergamum write:
These are the words of him who has the sharp, double-edged sword. [13]I know where you live—where Satan has his throne. Yet you remain true to my name. You did not renounce your faith in me, even in the days of Antipas, my faithful witness, who was put to death in your city—where Satan lives. [14]Nevertheless, I have a few things against you: You have people there who hold to the teaching of Balaam, who taught Balak to entice the Israelites to sin by eating food sacrificed to idols and by committing sexual immorality. [15]Likewise you also have those who hold to the teaching of the Nicolaitans. [16]Repent therefore! Otherwise, I will soon come to you and will fight against them with the sword of my mouth. [17]He who has an ear, let him hear what the Spirit says to the churches. To him who overcomes, I will give some of the hidden manna. I will also give him a white stone with a new name written on it, known only to him who receives it."

I. Introduction

Let us now look at the third church, the church at Pergamum. The dictation of the Lord was penned and sent to this church. As I have made clear from the beginning of this look at the early chapters of Revelation, these letters can apply literally to the churches to whom they are addressed, but they also apply practically to every church of Jesus Christ across all time and space. Most importantly, they apply to us, and more specifically, they apply to me and you individually as the Church of Jesus Christ.

The city of Pergamum was a capital of the region under Roman rule. It was the farthest north of the seven churches. It was actually the capital city of the kingdom of Pergamum, which was a great and flourishing kingdom in the time when John was writing this letter. This city was situated sixty-four miles north of Smyrna. Pergamum was a great political and religious center of the first century. It's been called both "the royal city" and "the city of authority." As the city grew in power and prestige, it also grew in many other ways, including a library with 200,000 volumes, a library second only to the one in Alexandria. This made Pergamum one of the great intellectual centers of its age as well. The Kingdom of Pergamum became a Roman province in 130 BC. Pergamum also rivaled Ephesus for being a center of world religions. There were temples to Zeus, Athena, and Dionysos. Next to one of these temples was the temple of Asklepios, the god of healing, called by many in that time, the god of Pergamum. The image of this particular god is still used on first aid emblems all around the world. Along with this focus on the god of healing, there also was a university for medical study.

Pergamum was the first city in Asia (A.D. 29) with a temple for the worship of Augustus, specifically, Octavius Caesar, and Pergamum, along with Smyrna, actually became the centers of emperor worship. Needless to say, the church at Pergamum faced great opposition. They were not merely in a satanic place, but, as the letter says, in the very seat of Satan. This reference was either given for the idol worship or the presence of the ungodly rule of Rome, either one of which or both would have been true of Pergamum. Revelation 17 speaks of a city on seven hills, and that would seem to point to the city. Whatever the cause of the name, the city was so wicked that the Lord said it was Satan's seat of rule. But the church also was in a very strategic place. Where else should the church of Jesus Christ be? We should be among those that hate the Gospel. We should be among those that choose darkness rather than light.

The world hates the Gospel, but we are IN the world, not OF the world. That's precisely what Jesus was praying for in His famous prayer for His disciples in John 17. As Jesus prayed, He prayed for His disciples until He came to verse 20, where He prayed for every one who would ever be redeemed. In His prayer, He reveals that the world would hate those who follow Him. It says in verses 13-20: "*I am coming to You now, but I say these things while I am still in the world, so that they may have the full measure of my joy within them. I have given them Your word and the world has hated them, for they are not of the world any more than I am of the world. My prayer is not that You take them out of the world but that you protect them from the evil one. They are not of the world, even as I am not of it. Sanctify them by the truth; Your word is truth. As you sent me into the world, I have sent them into the world. For them I sanctify myself, that they too may be truly sanctified. 'My prayer is not for them alone. I pray also for those who will believe in me through their message, that all of them may be one, Father, just as You are in me and I am in You. May they also be in Us so that the world may believe that You have sent me.'*"

This church dwelt in this wicked place, but they did so possessing the commission of the Lord. Our circumstances do not relieve us from our responsibility as children of God. The commission of Matthew 28:19-20 and Acts 1:8 were not made null and void for the church at Pergamum simply because they dwelt in a wicked place. Sometimes we want to relinquish our responsibility because the environment in which we live is just too tough, but God's command stands nonetheless.

II. The Letter to Pergamum

Let's now turn our attention to precisely what Jesus was saying to the Church at Pergamum and exactly what He is still saying to you and me as His church today. In verse 12, Jesus comes with "the sharp, double-edged sword." This sword, as we know, is the Word of God. It is an offensive weapon and it was designed to be used by the church, and it should be! The Word of God is for us. The Word of God is to us, but the Word of God does not belong to us, it is the possession of Jesus Christ. That is why we must handle the Word so very carefully. These days many people don't think much of watering down the Word and lowering its standards. As we approach the Word, we must never forget reverently and fearfully that it is God's Word, that it belongs to Him. We must carefully and prayerfully explore its teachings and share its truth, and never demean its value.

Many of the modern English translations have attempted to modernize the Word by omitting doctrinal verses or by making it "gender neutral" in order to satisfy the political correctness of our age.

Sadly, man has attempted to play God and has caused confusion instead of enhancing the study of the Word. Why has this happened? Too many of the modern handlers of the Word have forgotten precisely to Whom the Word of God belongs.

In Revelation 1:16, John tells us that "*in his right hand he held seven stars, and out of his mouth came a sharp double edged sword. His face was like the sun shining in all its brilliance.*" This double edged sword would cut at the very heart of the sin of the church.

In Hebrews 4:12, we see the Word of God described as "*living and active...sharper than any double-edged sword, it penetrates even to dividing soul and spirit, joints and marrow; it judges the thoughts and attitudes of the heart!*" We can read the Word, study the Word, teach the Word, and preach the Word, but it is not ours to do the work of the Word. It is the power of God's Word that changes and challenges us. It is the Word that strengthens the saints of the church. John had explained this in an earlier writing.

He says in 1 John 2:14, *"I write to you, fathers, because you have known Him who is from the beginning. I write to you, young men, because you are strong, and the Word of God lives in you, and you have overcome the evil one."* This writing, as all the writing of the Scripture, was under the inspiration of the Holy Spirit, and was for the benefit of the church, it was for the benefit of each of us as its members. It is to help us overcome the attempts of the wicked one to pull us away from the work that God has for us to do.

And as you can see, that is exactly what the church at Pergamum needed. It needed the Word to overcome Satan in that wicked place.

In the Lord's communication, we not only notice the Sword, but we notice His seeing.

To all seven churches, Jesus declares, *"I know your works."* When we are not faithful, He knows. When we serve Him half-heartedly, He knows. When we give in to the allures of our human nature, He knows. When we are totally sold out to His cause, He knows. The beginning of Psalm 139 says it well, *"O Lord, you have searched me and you know me. You know when I sit and when I rise, you perceive my thoughts from afar."* Jesus knows where we are in relation to Him, every minute of every day of our lives!

In verse 13, we see the stand they took. They were willing to be marked as Christ's followers. As we have seen previously, they did not shy away from being known as Christians. They were commended for holding fast the name of Christ, even in the face of great persecution. It would seem that the martyr who is mentioned, Antipas, was killed because he took issue with the wickedness of the city. Some believe a mob overtook him in the streets close to where the church met. Antipas was not named in any records of martyrs that I can find, which is significant in and of itself. It is so incredible to note that though the world may not see this martyr as one of notable historical reference, Jesus did. The faithful are noticed by Christ. The church was faithful not to deny the Lord. Most of the church did not waiver in their personal stand in Christianity, but there was a problem. The problem they had is one we should be familiar with in the church today.

In verse 14-15, we find that they sanctioned certain sins. They lowered their standard of righteousness by allowing some to remain in their midst who followed the same failures as Balaam. In Numbers 25 we see how Balaam persuaded Balak to deceive the Israelites to compromise on the standards of God and how that led the people to commit great sin before the Lord. Later in Numbers 31 we read additional compromise was found in Israel due to Balaam, where it says that the counsel of Balaam actually was responsible for the people of Israel trespassing against the Lord! The church at Pergamum was falling prey to the same kind of bad counsel the people of Israel had fallen prey to hundreds of years before. The church was allowing sexual impurity and idol worship. The church embraced the doctrine of tolerance. They gave into a system of compromise. And just to be clear, God did not simply dislike this doctrine, He hated it. What happened here was that the church had thrown away the teaching of Christ for the comforts of mankind. Let me say that again, the church has actually thrown away the teaching of Christ for the comforts of mankind! Ritual began to replace righteousness and desires replaced devotion to God.

There is a further connection between the doctrines of Balaam and the doctrines of the Nicolaitans and that was the problem of their abuse of their liberty in Christ. They were liberated from the law, but never free to sin. Galatians 5:13 tells us, "*You, my brothers, were called to be free. But do no use your freedom to indulge in the sinful nature, rather, serve one another in love.*" Paul continues in verse 16 to say, "*So I say, live by the Spirit, and you will not gratify the desires of the sinful nature.*"

A lawyer undertook the defense of a thief on the promise of a rich reward. He won his case, and his client brought him the coveted money. The night being stormy, the lawyer invited him to lodge in his house. At midnight the thief got up, gagged his legal defender, retook the money he gave him and, gathering all the treasure he could find, bid his helpless host good-bye. Such is the deceit of sin and the reward of iniquity. We can never make a friend of sin.

One other component of this letter is a component of each of the letters to the Churches. Each letter has an appeal to reach the lost.

The responsibility of the church is to reach the dying world with the Gospel. In verse 17 we see a promise of a heavenly feast, displayed as hidden manna. Jewish tradition says that when the Temple of Solomon was destroyed, Jeremiah took the manna that was in the ark of the Covenant and hid it in an unknown cave in a mountain, and when the Messiah comes, He would bring that hidden pot of manna out of the cave, BUT IT IS BETTER THAN THAT!

In John 6:49-51, Jesus taught, *Your forefathers ate the manna in the desert, yet they died. But here is the bread that comes down from heaven, which a man may eat and not die. I am the living bread that came down from heaven. If anyone eat of this bread, he will live forever. This bread is my flesh, which I will give for the life of the world."* Jesus reminds us that this Manna is only for those who overcome by the blood of the Lamb, different from the wilderness, this manna is the food reserved for the righteous.

There also is pardon offered for those who believe. This is seen in the white stone. In the Greek courts, judgment was given by two stones, a white stone and a black stone. If the judge found them guilty they would present a black stone, but if they were deemed innocent, the judge would cast a white stone of acquittal! When I trusted Christ as my Savior, I had a stone that was mine! And I have been made a stone unto God. Look at 1 Peter 2:4-5, it says, *"As you come to Him, the living Stone, rejected by men but chosen by God and precious to Him...you, also, like living stones, are being built into a spiritual house to be a holy priesthood, offering spiritual sacrifices acceptable to God through Jesus Christ."* This pardon is totally secure, the white stone of acquittal is actually engraved with my heavenly name forever.

I have a name that is my eternal name from God. Every child of God has this claim. The prophecy of Isaiah 56:5, says, *"to them I will give within my temple and its walls a memorial and a name better than sons and daughters; I will give them an everlasting name that will not be cut off."* This is wonderful security to the believer. The Lord names His own. Isaiah 62:2, speaks of this: *"The nations will see your righteousness, and all kings your glory; you will be called by a new name that the mouth of the Lord will bestow!"* It is sad to be sure, but this is something that the lost cannot understand, only those who will trust Christ alone for salvation will have a new name.

III. Conclusion

Pergamum was a church that did not denounce Christ, but dishonored him by their compromise. They would not deny the virgin birth or the resurrection, but beyond the majors, everything was minor. They where everything was OK. I am sometimes actually surprised we haven't seen a church established in our midst that is literally called the Church of Tolerance! In reality, those theologians and politicians that yell the loudest for tolerance are actually the most intolerant of all. Tolerance of sin is indifference. Indifference to sin will lead to blind corruption, and it has. When the church, or should we say, since the church has stepped into complacency and carnality, many will die without Christ. And remember to apply that truth to you personally, not simply to some nebulous manifestation called, "the church." Tolerance is a dangerous doctrine that has always existed.

I read a story that a boy was going down to the river for a little swim. As he was leaving the house his father said, *"Be careful, Herbert; the river looks fair and sparkling, but there is an ugly eddy beneath that may prove too much for you. I have tried it and know it is dangerous. It nearly overcame me. Be careful, son; there is danger."*

Herbert went on and was careful for a time, but the river looked so smooth and peaceful he soon ventured out farther. His companions, who were in bathing with him, admonished him to be careful. But he called back and said, *"I can swim; there is no danger."* So he ventured out still farther. But soon he was heard calling for help. The undercurrent had him. He frantically cried for assistance, but all in vain. He went down.

So it is with sin. It may look harmless, but there is the undercurrent. When we venture out, we will find that sin will take us deeper than we wanted to go and we will go down and, in going down, we dishonor the Lord. We, as His church, need to reject the so-called tolerance of today and get back to following the teachings and standards of the mighty double-edged Sword. Oh that we would not dishonor Christ by our tolerance!

Chapter 5
The Church That Can't Say No

What God Says to You as His Church

Revelation 2: 18-29

To the Church in Thyatira

[18]"To the angel of the church in Thyatira write:
These are the words of the Son of God, whose eyes are like blazing fire and whose feet are like burnished bronze. [19]I know your deeds, your love and faith, your service and perseverance, and that you are now doing more than you did at first. [20]Nevertheless, I have this against you: You tolerate that woman Jezebel, who calls herself a prophetess. By her teaching she misleads my servants into sexual immorality and the eating of food sacrificed to idols. [21]I have given her time to repent of her immorality, but she is unwilling. [22]So I will cast her on a bed of suffering, and I will make those who commit adultery with her suffer intensely, unless they repent of her ways. [23]I will strike her children dead. Then all the churches will know that I am he who searches hearts and minds, and I will repay each of you according to your deeds. [24]Now I say to the rest of you in Thyatira, to you who do not hold to her teaching and have not learned Satan's so-called deep secrets (I will not impose any other burden on you): [25]Only hold on to what you have until I come. [26]To him who overcomes and does my will to the end, I will give authority over the nations— [27]'He will rule them with an iron scepter; he will dash them to pieces like pottery'—just as

I have received authority from my Father. [28]I will also give him the morning star. [29]He who has an ear, let him hear what the Spirit says to the churches."

I. Introduction

As we continue our look at "What God Says to You as His Church," let's look back at what we have seen already. We have seen the church that needed to fall in love again, Ephesus. Simply put, they acted out of duty instead of love for the Lord. We saw the church that needed courage, the persecuted church at Smyrna. We also have looked at the church where anything goes, Pergamum. This church was a compromising church. In this chapter, we will look at the fourth church to whom Jesus dictated a letter through the Apostle John.

Thyatira, modern Akhisar, in Turkey, is located 42 miles inland from the Aegean Sea. It was noted for abundant crops, trade and the manufacture of a very costly purple dye. You may remember that one of Paul's first converts, Lydia, was a native of this city. She was saved at Philippi, seen in Acts 16:14. It says, "*One of those listening was a woman named Lydia, a dealer in purple cloth from the city of Thyatira, who was a worshiper of God. The Lord opened her heart to respond to Paul's message.*" Some Bible skeptics claim that there was no church in this city, because there is little in the way of archeological evidence to prove its existence.

But I have to ask the question, is it so hard to believe that Lydia and her family could have taken the Gospel back to their families?

However, there actually is historical evidence of a church in this city.

There are writings from church history that talk about a church from Thyatira that was overrun with false doctrine in the second century.

There also are footnotes to the annals of the ecumenical councils of the early church that actually record attendance by a bishop from Thyatira, specifically at the Council of Nicea in the fourth century.

So, we can assume from both a biblical perspective and an historical one that this church certainly did exist, just in case the archeologists cast any doubt! We also know that this church was sent a letter directly from Jesus, so what did He have to say?

II. The Letter

We see in verse 18 the communication, the Eternal Judge is speaking. He reiterates His deity by His title: He is the "Son of God." And He has the attributes of "eyes like blazing fire, and feet like burnished bronze." In Revelation 1:14-15, these two attributes are seen as Jesus is revealed to John and now they are used again. This description goes back to Daniel 10:6: *"His body was like chrsyolite, his face like lightening, his eyes like flaming torches, his arms and legs like the gleam of burnished bronze, and his voice like the sound of a multitude."* That's how Daniel described his own encounter with God. This is precisely how John described what he saw when he was granted this incredible vision of the Living Christ. And now, this is precisely how Jesus chooses to identify Himself as the Author of this letter.

We are left to analyze and arrive at some conclusions about what all that means. How about thinking of it this way? The eyes of God are a fire piercing through the rubbish of our lives searching out the hearts. This represents for us our understanding of the omniscience of Christ. His sight reaches to all persons and all things, His sight is searching and penetrating, it discovers and brings to light things the most dark and obscure. We read in 1 Corinthians 4:5, *"Therefore judge nothing before the appointed time; wait till the Lord comes. He will bring to light what is hidden in darkness and will expose the motives of men's hearts. At that time each will receive his praise from God."* His eyes will reveal all. I am reminded of 1 Corinthians 3, and the judgment seat of Christ. It says that *"Every man's work will be shown for what it is, because the Day will bring it to light. It will be revealed with fire, and the fire will test the quality of each man's work."* This is speaking to believers, our works will be revealed.

That day the judgment seat of Christ will reveal it. Why? It will be revealed by fire. Our works will be tried through the eyes of Jesus, and be revealed for what they really are. Oh that Jesus will help us to understand that fully, that nothing we think or do is hidden from our Father.

The fire also represents light. That shows us the love of Christ.

Jesus is the Light of the World. John 1:9 says that Jesus is *"the true Light that gives light to every man coming into the world."* What grace, that Jesus gives light to every man that comes into the world.

Every one who has ever been born will be without excuse when they stand before God. Scripture tells us that when anyone in the world accepts the light that they have been given that God will send them even more light. That is what the role of the church is supposed to be, this is what we are supposed to be, we are entrusted with the light and we are to take it to the lost.

If anyone in the world will accept the light that God has placed in all, God will send more light. Jesus is the light of the world, and in John 12:46 declared, *"I have come into the world as a light, so that no one who believes in me should stay in darkness."* Not only do we see the fire of His eyes, but we see the feet of God. They are made of fine bronze. Many believe this was an alloy of gold, silver, brass and copper that was blended to create a great brilliance. As I look at this, I see the feet of the Savior as the feet that bring good news. Isaiah saw Christ in this way as we read in Isaiah 52:7, that says, *"How beautiful on the mountains are the feet of Him who brings good news, who proclaim peace, who bring good tidings, who proclaim salvation; who say to Zion, Your God reigns!"* These feet that bring the good news, the Gospel of salvation, are feet that are to be worshiped.

It is at the feet of Jesus we find grace. It is at His feet we find mercy.

And it is at His feet that we should bow and offer our worship. Mary was found often at the feet of Jesus. When Jesus was in the house, Martha was busy, but Mary was comfortable at the feet of Jesus.

When Jesus approached them after Lazarus had died, Mary came and fell at His feet. Then in John 12:3, we see the great sacrifice of praise as "*Mary poured out an entire bottle of very costly perfume and anointed the feet of Jesus, and wiped his feet with her hair.*" He is worthy to be praised.

Not only are they feet of light and feet that bring the Gospel, but they are feet of judgment. His judgment will stand and there are none that have ever existed that can compete, challenge or question. Brass in the Bible tends to denote judgment. Think of the brazen altar. The sacrifices of the Old Testament were killed and offered on that altar of bronze. The judgment of God was held back, His wrath appeased as a sacrifice was offered on the altar of brass.

Next we see the commendation of the congregation. In verse 19, we see their tender love for Christ. "I know your love," He says. This is the Greek word, AGAPE, that wonderful word associated with the love of God, the total, unconditional love that God has for every single one of us! Jesus used that word to describe their love. They were fulfilling His commandment of John 15:12, that they, "love one another," just as Jesus had loved them.

In addition to commending them for their love, He commended them for their involvement in the ministry, He calls it their service.

True love will be followed by action. He commended their trust in God, they exhibited faith. Jesus acknowledged that He noticed their endurance, their suffering, as He noted their patience and continuing in the face of the trouble, He calls it their perseverance. They were not guilty as Ephesus, they had a love like their first love. Their last works were more, they were greater than their first works. The saved were going forward, BUT, there was a problem.

Jesus condemns them because of corruption in verses 20 through 23. They were allowing an unscriptural leader in their midst. There was a woman among them who had taken the mantle of leadership in a way that was not in keeping with the Scripture. This woman "called herself a prophetess." She was claiming a position to which she had no right. This unscriptural leader's problem wasn't because she was a woman, it was because she was not a true follower of Jesus, maybe that's why she is given the name Jezebel. To understand this, let us consider the Old Testament version of Jezebel. We must be careful what we call someone, because we are associating them with whom we call them. That's why nobody names their child Judas or Adolph anymore! Jezebel is considered by some to be the most evil woman who ever lived! The Jezebel of the Old Testament killed God's prophets. Is it possible, in Thyatira, that to keep her position, this Jezebel was actually allowing the persecution of certain Christians?

Many have compromised in order to keep their own power, that is not a far fetched conclusion to reach in this instance. We know that Jezebel openly went against God's man. It becomes apparent that she actually usurped leadership in that church and most definitely undermined the true leadership of the church, sowing great seeds of discord. Jezebel also set up idols. This could represent, not only physical idols, but idols of false doctrine.

This woman would be a forerunner of so called modern day "prophets and prophetesses" who usurp what the Bible teaches and stand in open opposition of the Scriptures. They come and set up prosperity and positive thinking type ministries, totally ignoring Biblical principles. One church right here in my own community actually claimed in their very mission statement that it is our God ordained right to be rich and that it is actually our mandate from God to pursue riches; another openly and blatantly promotes promiscuity and lifestyle choices clearly admonished in the Scripture. To do right at the expense of prosperity goes against their view of success, therefore they cast aside what the Bible says, they go against men and women of God, and in a sense allow the god of self satisfaction to permeate their teachings and those that follow them.

The Old Testament Jezebel was also a murderer. She went to great lengths to acquire the vineyard that Ahab coveted. She had Naboth murdered to advance her cause. She corrupted a nation. This woman that the church in Thyatira allowed to continue in their midst must have been doing the same things. Her sins included sexual immorality, this woman was dwelling in great wickedness, and the worst part of all is that she was not disciplined by the church, she was allowed to persist in leadership.

In verses 21 through 23, Jesus declared mercy, as He had given opportunity to this wicked woman, and to those who followed her, to repent. They had their chance, but refused, so now they will go through a period of intense suffering, and still God's goal in all of this is not punishment, but rather repentance! Eventually however, God's dealing with the lost, after an incredibly merciful time of opportunity, will be judgment and nothing less.

III. Conclusion

As we come to verses 24-29, we find a charge to those who are converted, a charge to the genuine Christians in their midst. Upon those who were not a part of this counterfeit religion, those that were truly saved, would face no judgment. They were to walk in the same faith that they already possessed. They were to "hold fast" in that which they already had received. This is not a keeping of our salvation, but rather it is a living out of our salvation. They were to remain faithful in the face of a perverted society.

This greatly speaks to us today. Even though we are live in a wicked society, we are to hold fast to the teachings and ways of our Lord, Jesus Christ. The church, you and me, are in so many ways today, giving in to the ways of the world. Simply put, God despises this. We are to stay faithful, and remember what is coming. God's people will reign with Him. We will have a part in His eternal Kingdom!

Verse 26 gives us the revelation that those who are faithful, those who hold fast, those who stand firm, will be given authority over all nations! The privilege of not only sharing the joys of eternal life, sharing possessions of Christ, we also will share His authority over all creation. We also will share the possessions of the Morning Star. Some may ask, what or who is this? Let Jesus tell us Himself. In Revelation 22:16, He said, *"I, Jesus, have sent my angel to give you this testimony for the churches. I am the Root and the Offspring of David, and the Bright Morning Star."* The Morning Star is the brightest star, and Jesus is the brightest light to mankind. His prophecies are sure, His way is perfect, His plan is established, and His pathway is lightened by His grace. Notice 2 Peter 1:19, as Peter declared, *"And we have the word of the prophets made more certain, and you will do well to pay attention to it, as to a light shining in a dark place, until the day dawns and the morning star rises in your hearts."*

This passage is talking about the word of God and when our faith is made sight, we will understand it all. It will be at that time that we will be in complete unity with the Morning Star!

He is mine and I am his now, but when this old body is redeemed, I will know Him like never before! Today I see in a mirror dimly, but then face to face, then I will know and I will enjoy the presence of the Morning Star forever. In thinking of this church from 2000 years ago, it must challenge us today to come to the decision that we must never tolerate sin, but rather live faithfully together for Christ until we see him face to face. It is then, in our glorified state that we will stand before the Lord in the brightness of His glory. Imagine all of God's children standing before Him. Our finite minds find it impossible to get a true grasp, but it is going to happen. We will be in the presence of the Almighty, the King of Kings.

The origination of the military salute is a simple story, but for me gives a glimpse of how we may react. After the defeat of the Spanish Armada in 1588, a naval tournament was arranged for the victorious British seamen and, at the request of Admiral Drake, Queen Elizabeth consented to come from London to award prizes. The officer in charge of arrangements issued orders that *"on account of the dazzling loveliness of her majesty, all men, upon receiving their prizes, should shield their eyes with their right hand."* As the Queen passed, each man lifted his hand as if to reduce the glare of her glory and thus was born the naval and military salute. Imagine as we face our Lord, and He approaches us with a crown that we may receive of His hand. As unworthy people we will be in the presence of the "dazzling loveliness" of the Majesty from on High. It will not be a mere earthly queen or ruler, but the King of Heaven, the Lord of all the ages. Possibly, we will have to salute as we face the splendor and brightness of the King. I can only imagine!

Chapter 6
The Church Without a Pulse

What God Says to You as His Church

Revelation 3: 1-6 (From the Message)

To Sardis
1 "Write this to Sardis, to the Angel of the church. The One holding the Seven Spirits of God in one hand, a firm grip on the Seven Stars with the other, speaks: 'I see right through your work. You have a reputation for vigor and zest, but you're dead, stone-dead.'
2-3 "Up on your feet! Take a deep breath! Maybe there's life in you yet. But I wouldn't know it by looking at your busywork; nothing of God's work has been completed. Your condition is desperate. Think of the gift you once had in your hands, the Message you heard with your ears—grasp it again and turn back to God.
'If you pull the covers back over your head and sleep on, oblivious to God, I'll return when you least expect it, break into your life like a thief in the night.
4 'You still have a few followers of Jesus in Sardis who haven't ruined themselves wallowing in the muck of the world's ways. They'll walk with me on parade! They've proved their worth!
5 'Conquerors will march in the victory parade, their names indelible in the Book of Life. I'll lead them up and present them by name to my Father and his Angels.
6 'Are your ears awake? Listen. Listen to the Wind Words, the Spirit blowing through the churches.'"

I. Introduction

I read the other day about a company that makes blank bumper stickers. They're for people who don't want to get involved and don't want to offend anyone. That's how so many religious groups in our day have decided to approach things of faith. So-called preachers place their voices on the airways, admitting that they do not deal with sin because they don't want to be negative, that people don't want to hear that kind of stuff.

Friends, we are living in an awesome time because we know that Jesus is coming soon, there appears to be little doubt of that. Yet we are living in a very dangerous and sad time, seeing so many who claim to be "spiritual," but are in fact, denying the power and principles of God's ways.

Now we turn our attention to the fifth church in our survey of the churches of Revelation, the church in Sardis. So far in our survey of these churches, I haven't dealt with the prophetic applications of the letters, but want to put just a small portion in at this point in our discussion. Remember how I told you that the letters could be viewed in three distinct ways: as actual letters to actual first century churches, as letters to all churches at all times, and they also can be viewed prophetically, where each church is representative of a specific period of church history between the time of the Cross and the return of the Lord. In prophetic terms then, it is believed that Thyatira represented the Dark Ages. And from the Dark Ages there emerged a remnant. From that remnant of saved people came the Reformation. Theologians tell us that Sardis represented the time that led us into the Reformation. The world was changing. A new emphasis on the study of the Bible began with the invention of the printing press. A few, the remnant, stood in opposition to the false doctrines of the Jezebels of their own time. Yet it fell short of what could have been achieved. It is an historical fact, that the church of the reformation, seen by many as a church of rebellion, actually has produced for the world its greatest understanding of Bible doctrines. So many began to reveal truth and yet their doctrines were attacked as heresy. The Orthodoxy of that day created such complacency with the way things were that made those who questioned the status quo to be seen as heretics and rabble rousers. Those who wished to bring truth to light, to bring attention to the false teaching of the day and to expose the carnality running rampant in the church were denounced as traitors and devil worshippers. This particular understanding is crucial to our view of this letter and to the specifics of what God has to say to us through His church in Sardis. So let's now turn our attention to that little church.

Sardis was a city that was about thirty miles southeast of Thyatira. It was known as one of the great trade centers of the world. It was a wealthy city. It was an industrious city and Sardis was the greatest distributor of wool in the world at that time. At the same time it was a wicked city. History tells us that the inhabitants were pleasure seeking and loose in their living. It is said that the name Sardis became a byword for immoral living. This church wasn't persecuted like some of the others we've looked at, rather it was a complacent church.

Historians actually described Sardis as *"the city of Death, a city of softness and luxury, of apathy and immorality..."* Complacency has a way of doing that. Complacency saps energy and dulls attitudes. The first symptom is satisfaction with things as they are. The second is rejection of things as they might be. "Good enough" becomes today's watchword and tomorrow's standard. Complacency makes people fear the unknown, mistrust the untried, and hate the new. Like water, complacent people follow the easiest course and it's always downhill. And mankind is often as unstable as water. We naturally follow the path of least resistance and, without Christ, will end up at the lowest point. A dead ritual leads to a dead religion every time. And dead religion produces no fruit.

II. The Letter

This was a message from the Redeemer. John was penning the words, but they were from God. God the Father, God the Son, and God the Holy Spirit are one God. They have always been, evermore shall be, and always are one. Seven is the number of completion, and this is the fulfillment of Christ having the fullness of the Spirit of God upon Him. It is written that this was *"the fullness and perfection of the gifts and grace of the Spirit of God."* God is one, yet is manifested to us in the three persons of the God-Head. Seven Spirits speaks of the fullness of the Spirit of God. The sevenfold fullness of the Spirit of God that rests upon Jesus is found in Isaiah 11:2-3. It says, *"The Spirit of the Lord will rest on Him...the Spirit of wisdom and of understanding, the Spirit of counsel and of power, the Spirit of knowledge and of the fear of the Lord...and He will delight in the fear of the Lord. He will not judge by what He sees with His eyes, or decide by what He hears with His ears..."*

It was prophesied that the Spirit would rest upon the Messiah. This was a permanent resting that will not just come upon Him, but was there eternally. There are seven things that relate between the Spirit and the Messiah in this prophecy. There is wisdom, understanding (discernment), counsel, power, knowledge, and the fear of the Lord (that which demands reverence). The seventh attribute says the Spirit would "make him of righteous in His judgment" The word "righteous" interestingly is translated "smell" eight times in the Old Testament. It literally means that the seventh work of the Spirit was to make Him a sweet smell to others.

Here's lesson number one for us in this Letter: We cannot be the church, we cannot be the followers we are designed to be without the fullness of the Spirit of God!

Notice next: Jesus is the One who has the seven stars. He is the Head of the Church, He is the ultimate authority. As a pastor, I have trouble when people say: "Tell me about 'your' church" or "How's 'your' church doing?" It's not "MY" church, it's His church, we are the sheep of His pasture, we are His flock. So many, especially in our day and age, become arrogant and act as if they are building their own kingdoms. As members of His church, we are not building our kingdoms, we are serving in His. He is the head and He is the authority over all. Colossians 1:18 declares, *"And He is the head of the body, the church; He is the beginning and the firstborn from among the dead, so that in everything He might have the supremacy."* The stars are the pastors of the seven churches. He has them in His hand. This is a picture that these pastors were God's men. Each pastor is greatly and personally accountable to Christ and Christ alone. This is a fearful position, abused by many, and subject to the greatest accountability. I'm not saying that a pastor is not accountable to his flock and other pastors. But what I am saying is that in contrast with the accountability of a pastor to Christ, all other accountability is as nothing. Human accountability pales in the light of the accountability that the leadership of a church has to Christ.

In verse one of chapter three, we see a rebuke. Again, Jesus declares, "I know thy deeds." The other four churches, up to this point, were commended first, but not Sardis. He told them that they had made a name for themselves, they had a reputation. The church had a true remnant and they were reported as famous for their faith and their diligence. They had every appearance of a vibrant and growing church, but they had a problem, the church as a whole was dead. What a horrible thing to have said about you by the One who holds you in His hand! What it meant was that the majority of the people in the church were probably lost and that even the remnant had a dead faith to the world because they were not living lives consistent with what they claim to believe! Their faith, without suitable works, was dead! And that made them no better than hypocrites. They needed to learn the rudimentary teachings of the book of James. The seventeenth verse of the second chapter of the book of James says, *"In the same way, faith by itself, if it is not accompanied by action, is dead!"* It has been explained away in a wide variety of ways, but it is hard to escape the truth that a large portion of the Sardis church was lost.

There was a reaction that Jesus wanted from them. They had been rebuked, now, in verse two, a response is expected. They were to "WAKE UP," to be watchful, to be vigilant and alert. The sleeping church needed to awaken to righteousness. They were to strengthen things that were alive, even if they are just barely alive! They needed a fresh diligence. They were to be thorough in their works. Their works were not what they should be. They were imperfect, and incomplete before Him. This could be a picture of unfaithful believers, or some that were not believers at all. The church is admonished to remember. They were not to throw away the things that they knew were right.

In verse 3, they are to call to mind the things that they had been taught. It was necessary for them to give attention to sound doctrine.

This church was to hold fast, that is, they were to obey the things they knew already, they didn't need to learn anything else, simply return to what they already knew! As His Church, that is our personal instruction! In Hebrews 2:1, we read, *"We must pay more careful attention, therefore, to what we have heard, so that we do not drift away!"* This remembrance would lead them to repentance. They needed to get back to the Truth and WAKE UP! Simply put, it is crystal clear that God despises a church that's dead!

It seems to me that what God is saying is that dead people that fill the pews of churches are not genuine believers and actually become the means by which others are brought down with them! When we're not living for Him, when we are dead spiritually, one of the first places that it shows up is in our Worship of Him. Failure to have worship that is alive and vibrant is an early detection devise for what's happening in our hearts!

In addition our theology needs to be alive. Our doxology needs to be alive! All our "ologies" need to have the life of Christ in them. He must be in the center of it all and the worldliness of modern times must be rejected. We need to proclaim as loudly as we can: *"I refuse to be a dead, dry, going through the motions, dread going to church, back-sliden Christian.* The danger that this letter points out is that some are lost and just going through the motions, while some are saved but dried up on the vine. Repentance is needed in either case!

And Jesus tells us that there were a few in Sardis, a small group of godly saints, a few that did not soil their clothes! God has always, and will always have a people. They had garments that were undefiled. When I think of that, my mind goes to the soldier in uniform. The uniform is pressed and all elements of it are in place. It's the very picture of service, commitment and obedience! There were some who did not defile themselves by unbelieving. They were not guilty of an unbecoming walk. They could not be accused of a denial of Christ or embracing false doctrines. This remnant was promised an eternal fellowship of walking with the Lord. We must remember that we do not only walk with the Lord by faith in this present time, but we are going to take a stroll across eternity with Jesus. The saved are made worthy to do this. We are not worthy ourselves, not by works, but worthy because we have been genuinely redeemed by the blood of the Lamb. And catch this: genuinely saved people are not religious, they're redeemed.

There is much controversy in the media and many skeptics of Christianity like to ask us if someone believes that a Muslim or Jew will go to heaven. The answer is very simple. A Muslim, Jew, Hindu, Mormon, Baptist, Methodist, or pagan can all go to heaven the same way. Jesus Christ is the only way to heaven. It is not religion or affiliation that redeems, but faith solely in Jesus and His death, burial and resurrection. Any less for any person will bring damnation. Jesus declared this in His own words in John 14:6, as He declared to Thomas, *"I am the way, the truth and the life, no one comes to the Father, but by Me."* What more can be said, Jesus is the only way. The Jewish tradition has a saying somewhat like this, *"they that walk with God in their lifetime, 'are worthy' to walk with him after their death."* In 2 Thessalonians 1:3-5, we read this: *"We ought always to thank God for you, brothers, and rightly so, because your faith is growing more and more, and the love every one of you has for each other is increasing. Therefore, among God's churches we boast about your perseverance and faith in all the persecutions and trials you are enduring. All this is evidence that God's judgment is right, and as a result you will be counted worthy of the kingdom of God, for which you are suffering."*

This manifest token is the proof of God's work in our lives. It is only by the work of God that we can be counted worthy of the kingdom of God. Not only is there a remnant, but there is a rejoicing. The lost have nothing over which they can rejoice. We will rejoice that we are robed in white. White raiment was used among the Romans as a token of joy at festivals, on birthdays, at weddings, and times of great celebration. It gives a glimpse of the imputed righteousness of Christ. The saved are pure in Him. Also, the name of the righteous is in the book of life. An indication of some being blotted out is evident. Though many books are mentioned, it seems clear that some are blotted out of this book, so who are? All who die without Christ will die the second death, that is, they will not exist as far as God is concerned. They will not be in any of His books.

This is simple when you consider Jewish traditions. A custom among the Jews and Gentiles of registering the inhabitants of the city. All that were born were put in the book, and when they died, they were taken out of the book. Jesus never blots His redeemed out of the book, only those who die without Him. We are not saved by works so we cannot earn a spot in the book. We do not keep our spot by works. This is the book of life, the list of all for whom Christ died!

At some point, all humanity, all who have possessed life, the inhabitants of the world are in the book. Again, to make the point clear, when a person dies, if they have not received Christ, their name is blotted out, or wiped away, out of the book. When a person is saved, their name is confirmed in that book forever and their name is "confessed" or acknowledged openly and joyfully. Plainly stated, the only ones who will remain in this book are those who trust Christ and have heavenly citizenship.

III. Conclusion

All this begs the question, a question that must be asked, Am I a child of God? Is your name there, or will you reject Him and your name be blotted out? If you are saved, are you dead in your faith, only living through the motions?

I read a story about a great conductor. Sir Michael Costa was conducting a rehearsal in which the orchestra was joined by a great chorus. About halfway through the session, with trumpets blaring, drums rolling, and violins singing their rich melody, the piccolo player muttered to himself, "*What good am I doing? I might as well not be playing. Nobody can hear me anyway.*" So he placed his instrument to his lips but made no sound. Within moments the conductor cried, "*Stop! Stop! Where's the piccolo?*" Perhaps many people did not realize that the piccolo was missing, but the most important one did.

So it is in the Christian life. God knows when we do not play the part assigned to us, even if others do not. We must not be dead in our walk with Christ. May our lives be real, evident and vibrant in this realm as we serve the Lord.

Chapter 7
The Rockin' Church

What God Says to You as His Church

Revelation 3: 7-13

To the Church in Philadelphia

[7]"To the angel of the church in Philadelphia write:
These are the words of him who is holy and true, who holds the key of David. What he opens no one can shut, and what he shuts no one can open. [8]I know your deeds. See, I have placed before you an open door that no one can shut. I know that you have little strength, yet you have kept my word and have not denied my name. [9]I will make those who are of the synagogue of Satan, who claim to be Jews though they are not, but are liars—I will make them come and fall down at your feet and acknowledge that I have loved you. [10]Since you have kept my command to endure patiently, I will also keep you from the hour of trial that is going to come upon the whole world to test those who live on the earth. [11]I am coming soon. Hold on to what you have, so that no one will take your crown. [12]Him who overcomes I will make a pillar in the temple of my God. Never again will he leave it. I will write on him the name of my God and the name of the city of my God, the new Jerusalem, which is coming down out of heaven from my God; and I will also write on him my new name. [13]He who has an ear, let him hear what the Spirit says to the churches."

I. Introduction

This city of Philadelphia was located about 28 miles southeast of Sardis. It was a place noted for its agricultural products, but it also was a place afflicted with earthquakes. In A.D. 17, while under the reign of Tiberius, it almost totally was destroyed by an earthquake.

Perhaps because of this, the church in Philadelphia never attained the level of prominence that some of the other churches we have looked at had in their day. That the church itself was poor and wanting in worldly endowments seems to be indicated by verse 8. This church and that of Smyrna alone escape criticism from the Lord.

Its name means "brotherly love," as is commonly known due to the city in Pennsylvania that bears the same name. The same word "Philadelphia" is found in the Scriptures in 5 other verses. Consider Romans 12:10: *"Be devoted to one another in brotherly love."* Paul, Peter, and the writer to the Hebrews all share these same thoughts.

What a beautiful name for the church that was so commended by Christ. God loves to see His church, His people, loving one another.

God loves unity. We notice the truth of this in Psalm 133:1, that says, *"How good and pleasant it is when brothers live together in unity!"*

Then, in John 15:12, Jesus declared, *"My command is this: Love each other as I have loved you."* Paul wrote in Philippians 2:2, *"...then make my joy complete by being like-minded, having the same love, being one in spirit and purpose!"* God loves unity among His people. Children of God have no cause to be against one another.

Jealousy has no place in the church. Bitterness is a cancer that will not only hurt the church, but is one that will wreck individual lives.

God wants His church to be a church of "brotherly love."

Oh, how I needed to hear this message from God, the time could not be any more powerful as we arrive at this Letter to the Church of "brotherly love."

II. The Letter

Once again, let us look at this letter from the perspective that the letters address the various eras of Church history. At the beginning of the 19th century there was a dramatic change. The fervent focus and hope for the return of Christ had been thoroughly neglected and was virtually unknown by the masses of church members. But then the truth of the Lord's imminent return was revived. The Church awoke as well and the Gospel began to be preached unlike it had been since the beginning of the church. Names like Whitfield, Wesley, and Edwards set the stage for those to come later, like Moody and Spurgeon. The Deadness of Sardis began to disappear with the solid, doctrinal, Biblical preaching of these men and others.

This age reaches to us today. It is my belief, that if we were to try to locate ourselves in the place in Church history represented by these letters, that we are living in an overlap of the periods of Philadelphia and Laodicea. We will deal with Laodicea soon enough.

As the church at Philadelphia is addressed, we once again see Christ, the Author, describe Himself to His church. He is holy. We read in Isaiah 6:3 as Isaiah comes face to face with the God of the Universe and describes for us what he is witnessing, *"And they were calling to one another: 'Holy, holy, holy is the Lord Almighty; the whole earth is full of His glory."* It is interesting to note that the only attribute of God that is ever mentioned in this way is His holiness. We don't find "love, love, love" or "grace, grace, grace." Yet we find "holy" listed to the third power. God's holiness is the essence of His being and His character. His holiness greatly attaches to the next attribute that is named.

Jesus is Truth. In 1 John 5:20, the Apostle John had already penned, *"We know also that the Son of God has come and has given us understanding, so that we may know Him who is True. And we are in Him who is true...even in His Son Jesus Christ. He is true God and eternal life."* The fact is that there is no truth aside from Jesus Christ.

Though so many today simply will not believe in absolutes, it doesn't really matter because there still are absolutes regardless of the public opinion polls! Absolute truth is Jesus alone. It is just as John 1:17 says, *"... grace and truth came through Jesus Christ."*

In verse 7, we also see a possession that belongs to Jesus. He owns the keys to the Kingdom. A key is a symbol of trust, power, right of access, and even ownership. I would not give a key for my house to someone I didn't trust or that I hadn't given permission to go into my house! This key is the key of David which was prophesied in Isaiah, which is as clear a reference to the Messiah as there is in the Old Testament and speaks boldly of Christ's power over eternity! In Revelation 1:18, we find the reference to the "keys" in the Lord's possession. It says, *"I am the Living One; I was dead, and behold I am alive forever and ever! And I hold the keys of death and Hades."*

The key to salvation is in Christ alone. The key to supplication is only through Christ. The key to real satisfaction is only in Christ. And the keys of deliverance from eternal separation from God belong to One and only One, and that is Jesus Christ. Many think they have salvation and deliverance due to some human goodness or religious affiliation. Let me say this as clearly as I can, if it is not of Christ, it is of no value whatsoever as it relates to salvation!

In verse 8, we see the opportunity, an open door before the church, an open door for believers. In the realm of the prophetic application, this could easily represent England and America and the missions endeavors around the world. Today, we have an open door of freedom. Though we are attacked by anti-God groups on every side, we still enjoy wonderful freedom. Freedom is not the right to do nothing, nor does it mean to do as you please. The freedom the Scripture describes came with a price, it came through the blood of Jesus. With that freedom comes responsibility. We have an open door before us. An open door to witness and send the Gospel around the world. I'm sorry to say as I look over our evangelical landscape, that we have neglected our freedom in America. We have an open door of evangelism, yet we fall prey to the many who say that we should not confront others with the story of Jesus Christ.

The Bible tells us a different story. The Bible gives us a different approach. The Bible talks of Paul, one who was faithful to take these open doors in his time. In 2 Corinthians 2:12, he said, *"Now when I went to Troas to preach the gospel of Christ and found that the Lord had opened a door for me..."*

We have the open doors of world-wide missions. How powerful a time it was for the Church I was serving when God first placed it on my heart, it was a Sunday when one of our missions teams was working in West Virginia and another was preparing to leave for Haiti. This door is an open door to the church, and the church of Philadelphia had an open door before them, so what is the church to do? What are we to do? The church must face the challenge. We must face the challenge.

In verse eight it says that they had a "little strength." Some believe that they were small in number, while others say this had to do with their political and social influence, probably both! Compared with the other churches they were not as big or as glamorous. They may not have had ample financial supply or strength in numbers, but they had strength in God. In spite of everything they were faithful! They kept His Word in a time when others had not. Keeping the Word of the Lord is a clear indication of just how much we get it! By keeping His Word, the people in that little church in Philadelphia not only declared their love for Christ, they demonstrated it by their lives. In the face of adversity, they did not deny Him as so many others had. A bogus believer has no problem denying the Lord when it becomes inconvenient to live the Christian life. And it is precisely that level of hypocrisy that has been the very example drawn upon by many who refuse to answer the call of salvation when it is offered to them.

This church was different! This church was genuine, they had not denied the Lord. Once He states that, Jesus goes on to identify the imposters in an even greater way. He begins to speak of some who would divide the church. These imposters were Jews who stood against Christianity. Some infiltrated the church and caused problems, but unlike some of the others, this church was not the problem. Just to be clear, while Jesus is speaking of the specific situation that is happening in Philadelphia, He also is speaking to us.

He is referring to all false and hypocritical professors of the faith, those who would claim to be a member of the Church while all the while working feverishly to divide it! Those who practice hating, maligning, and opposing those who would keep the gospel. In the fourth verse of the book of Jude, a warning is given. Jude wrote, *"For certain men whose condemnation was written about long ago have secretly slipped in among you. They are godless men, who change the grace of our God into license for immorality and deny Jesus Christ our only Sovereign and Lord."* These people were against the church and what it was doing, but the day will come that they will yield. They will bow, they will acquiesce to the church. Some believe that this means that the house of Israel that rejected the Gospel will bow before the church. Others believe this is a reference to Messianic Jews who will trust Christ as their Savior, rejecting those who refuse to see Jesus as the Messiah. Either way, the church will still be standing when the smoke of time clears.

Jesus loves His church, so therefore, a truth upon which we can firmly stand is this, the church will always be loved. The rejecters of the Truth will know that He has loved a Gentile church! I love the security of Romans 8. In verse 35, the question is asked, *"Who shall separate us from the love of Christ? Shall trouble or hardship or persecution or famine or nakedness pr danger or sword?"* And then the great answer is given in verses 37-39: *"No, in all these things we are more than conquerors through Him who loved us. For I am convinced that neither death nor life, neither angels nor demons, neither the present nor the future, nor any powers, neither height nor depth, nor anything else in all of creation will be able to separate us from the love of God that is in Christ Jesus our Lord!"* To this the church must respond with a glorious "hallelujah" and a heart-felt "Amen!" AMEN?

We are His and we belong to Him forever. We may be of little strength, but when Christ possesses us we will stand for Him and live with Him as eternity rolls.

In verse 10, we find an irrefutable promise to this church. It is a promise to those who have not only heard the Gospel, but have also received it. They have "kept" His word with patience. The word "kept" means that they had given attention to, observed, guarded or taken care of His words. They gave their full attention to the Lamb of God.

They had given their full attention to His redemption plan, they belonged to the Lord. And as a result a promise is given that they would be kept from the hour of trial that would come upon the whole world.

Verses 11-12 are a promise to the over-comer. This speaks of those that are possessors of victory. We have and we do overcome by the blood of Jesus. We are more than conquerors through Him.

In speaking to the saved, the warning is given, not to be concerned about losing salvation, but losing rewards. For the faithful, a picture of being a pillar in the Temple of God is painted. Imagine that as the faithful saints of God, we have an eternal heavenly status due to our earthly faithfulness. A pillar is something that supports something. It also can be a part of architecture that adds beauty. These pillars were to be in the temple of God—the new Jerusalem!

How do we become those pillars? We must be pillars in the church. There are those who LIFT and those who LEAN. The lifters are the Pillars. Prayer, service, attitude, unity, support, loving one another, tithing, giving, witnessing, and anything else you can find to do to lift the church will bring an eternal reward of being a pillar! Do we hold up the church through the power of God or would it fall if it depended on you? Are you a lifter or a leaner? I can tell you without hesitation that there is nothing like serving the Lord. There is no greater calling than to be a preacher of the Gospel. All will not be called to be pastors, but we are all called to preach with our lives, we are all called to be those that lift up the work of God.

A brilliant young man with a magnetic personality went out to the mission field. His salary was minute. A large commercial firm was so eager to obtain his services that they offered him ten times his salary, but he refused. They offered to make it even larger if he would accept. They asked him if the money was not enough, and told him that if he would leave the mission field and come to work at their company, they would pay his price. He responded, "*Oh, the salary is big enough,*" he told them, "*but the job isn't!*" How I wish I'd thought of that! We should desire to be faithful lifters to the work of God.

These pillars are those that have been purchased by God. They will be positioned by God. And God will put His name, in fact He will engrave His name on them forever. We will be identified with the Almighty forever! Praise God from Whom that blessing flows!

Chapter 8
"The Church Under Attack"

What God Says to You as His Church

John 15:20

[20] *Remember the words I spoke to you: 'No servant is greater than his master.'* [a] *If they persecuted me, they will persecute you also. If they obeyed my teaching, they will obey yours also."*

Prior to one of our Haiti missions trips in 1998, we had been working through the 7 letters to the 7 churches of Revelation and learning what God was saying to OUR church through these letters. I had one church left to look at when we returned from that trip, but I was not quite ready to finish the series by returning to the final church, and I am not quite ready to go to the last church yet either. Instead I would like return to the scene of one of the church's we have already looked at and take a closer look at what God is saying to each one of us today!

Revelation 2: 8-11

To the Church in Smyrna

[8]"To the angel of the church in Smyrna write:

These are the words of him who is the First and the Last, who died and came to life again. [9]I know your afflictions and your poverty—yet you are rich! I know the slander of those who say they are Jews and are not, but are a synagogue of Satan. [10]Do not be afraid of what you are about to suffer. I tell you, the devil will put some of you in prison to test you, and you will suffer persecution for ten days. Be faithful, even to the point of death, and I will give you the crown of life. [11]He who has an ear, let him hear what the Spirit says to the churches. He who overcomes will not be hurt at all by the second death.

I. Introduction

Every November, many evangelical churches mark an International Day of Prayer for the Persecuted Church around the world and it is incumbent on all of us as His children to pay particularly close attention to the persecuted church wherever it exists in the world. God is definitely saying something to us about our brothers and sisters all over the world that are suffering for their faith in Jesus Christ. Alarming reports are streaming in from all over today's world, believers in many countries are being tortured and even killed because of their stand for Jesus.

God wants us to know that an attack upon any part of His body is an attack upon every part of the body because it is an attack upon Christ with whom we all are inextricably linked. Interestingly enough, there is no Biblical model to endure persecution if one has the ability and power to do something about it. Peter in Acts 5 is released from prison in order to continue to preach the Word of God. Paul in Acts 16 is praising God from His shackles and the shackles fall off, not so he could escape, but so that he could reach more for Christ. Paul in Acts 25 is given the supernatural power to simply stand up before one of the most powerful man in world and preach the Gospel and he would have released him on the spot had Paul not demanded to be sent to Rome.

Persecution of the church is something that always has been a part of church history and it is something that we need to continue to address, even though it is something that is so foreign to us in the United States that we may think of it as ancient history.

II. Facts of the Persecuted Church

Let's begin our exploration of the Persecuted Church with some amazing and alarming facts about the persecuted church in the 21st century. More than 160,000 believers were martyred in 2007, and countless others were subjected to unimaginable horrors. There were close to 100 million martyrs in the so-called "modern" 20th century. There were more people martyred for their faith in Jesus Christ in the 20th century than in all the previous nineteen combined. More people have died in circumstances related to their faith in this century than in all the 20th century wars combined. Pakistan recently passed a blasphemy law that forbids speaking or acting against the prophet Mohammed. The punishment for violators is death. A 12-year-old Christian child was recently sentenced to death under this law and was freed from Pakistan only by international pressure. He is now hiding in a Western country with a bounty on his head. The United Nations reports that the militant Islamic government of central African Sudan has undertaken a systematic battle against Christians. Since 1982, 300,000 Sudanese Christians have been killed. Each year hundreds of Christian believers are sold into slavery and taken where they have to work as slaves or as concubines for their Muslim masters. Lai Man Peng was a 22-year-old Chinese Christian evangelist. At a meeting of one of China's "house churches" (a non-government-sanctioned prayer meeting), he and four other evangelists were seized by agents of the Public Security Bureau, China's KGB. In front of the congregation, Mr. Lai and the others were beaten severely. The security officers next handed the rods to the congregants and ordered them to beat the preachers, on pain of being beaten themselves. Mr. Lai was so badly injured that the security team feared he would die in their presence (leaving too much to explain), so they released him. He crawled and hobbled for several miles attempting to reach his home, but finally collapsed and died on the road. Such persecution is commonplace in China, where only a fraction of the estimated 30 million to 70 million Christians belong to government-approved sects.

Amnesty International reports cases of Christian women hung by their thumbs from wires and beaten with heavy rods, denied food and water and shocked with electric probes.

Why is this happening? Is this a new occurrence? What does the Bible say about the persecution of Christians? What are the responsibilities of believers like us who may not be facing the same type of persecution at this time?

III. Why Is the Church Persecuted?

Persecution of the Church today is the same as it has always been, it is precisely the same as it was for the little church in Smyrna that faced the horrors of the Roman Empire. The first thing we need to know is that the persecution of the church is directed by Satan. It is Satan's way of attempting to usurp God's authority. 1 Peter 5:8 reminds us of this: *"Be self-controlled and alert. Your enemy the devil prowls around like a roaring lion looking for someone to devour."* Satan is seeking to devour believers—devour in the Greek means to swallow or destroy. The second thing we need to know about persecution is that, regardless of its origins, it can be used by God to strengthen the church. It is one of God's methods of strengthening His children. James actually begins his letter this way: *"James, a servant of God and of the Lord Jesus Christ, to the twelve tribes scattered among the nations: Greetings. Consider it pure joy, my brothers, whenever you face trials of many kinds, because you know that the testing of your faith develops perseverance. Perseverance must finish its work so that you may be mature and complete, not lacking anything. If any of you lacks wisdom, he should ask God, who gives generously to all without finding fault, and it will be given to him."* When our faith is tested it produces endurance in our walk with the Lord that will be necessary for us to finish the race!

The next thing we need to know about persecution is that it is part of the destiny of those who stand for Jesus! Persecution is the direct result of our stand for Jesus says the apostle Paul. In his second letter to Timothy he writes, *"In fact, everyone who wants to live a godly life in Christ Jesus will be persecuted.*" (2 Tim. 3:12) The awesome result of our stand for Jesus is our ultimate reward: The crown of righteousness. In 2 Tim. 4:7-8 Paul says, "*I have fought the good fight, I have finished the race, I have kept the faith. Now there is in store for me the crown of righteousness, which the Lord, the righteous Judge, will award to me on that day—and not only to me, but also to all who have longed for his appearing.*" Those who live godly lives will be persecuted. It is not an option.

IV. What Are the Biblical Examples of Persecution?

We heard a little bit about some modern day examples of persecution that are taking place right now. How about some of the Biblical examples that God has recorded for our benefit? There is that incredible story of Daniel and the lion's den found in Daniel 6.

In light of pending persecution, Daniel did not alter his godly lifestyle.

Even when "push came to shove," Daniel persevered; he trusted God in life or death. His reward: "*No wound was found on him because he trusted his God.*" How about the Apostle Paul? Paul viewed persecution as a constant reminder of his weakness. Through persecution Paul recognized his utter dependency on God. His reward as found in 2 Corinthians 12:8-10: "*Three times I pleaded with the Lord to take it away from me. But he said to me, "My grace is sufficient for you, for my power is made perfect in weakness."*

Therefore I will boast all the more gladly about my weaknesses, so that Christ's power may rest on me. That is why, for Christ's sake, I delight in weaknesses, in insults, in hardships, in persecutions, in difficulties. For when I am weak, then I am strong."

How about the Roll Call of the faithful found in Hebrews 11? What we learn from this incredible litany of the heroes of the faith is that our focus is not to be on the temporal, the stuff that's here today and gone tomorrow, rather our focus needs to be on the eternal, those things which never change! The opening verses tell a great story: *"Now faith is being sure of what we hope for and certain of what we do not see. This is what the ancients were commended for. By faith we understand that the universe was formed at God's command, so that what is seen was not made out of what was visible."* Faith in the Lord is the bottom-line of our S.O.P. [Standard Operating Procedure].

Verse 6 of Hebrews 11 goes on to say, *"And without faith it is impossible to please God, because anyone who comes to him must believe that he exists and that he rewards those who earnestly seek him."* Through faith, through standing firm in the midst of trial and temptation, we are able to desire something "better" than this world has to offer.

Verse 16 says, *"Instead, they were longing for a better country—a heavenly one. Therefore God is not ashamed to be called their God, for he has prepared a city for them."* Through faith, through standing firm we are able to determine for ourselves what we already know to be true, God is able to do whatever He says He will do, whether we understand it or not!

Verse 19 tell us that *"Abraham reasoned that God could raise the dead, and figuratively speaking, he did receive Isaac back from death."* Through faith, through standing firm in our trials and in the face of persecution we are able to get a glimpse of our eternal reward. Listen to verses 39 & 40, *"These were all commended for their faith, yet none of them received what had been promised. God had planned something better for us so that only together with us would they be made perfect."*

What about the first martyr in the church, Stephen in Acts 7? Listen to this from verses 57 & 58, *"At this they covered their ears and, yelling at the top of their voices, they all rushed at him, dragged him out of the city and began to stone him. Meanwhile, the witnesses laid their clothes at the feet of a young man named Saul."* In this story two amazing things happen. Stephen remains steadfast throughout and actually begins to pray for those throwing the stones! As a result of his witness, he is welcomed in Heaven by Jesus Himself. Catch this: Where is Jesus today? He is seated at the right hand of God, right? Well, what does it say in verse 56? He saw Jesus "standing at the right hand of God!" That means that Jesus stood up, got up off His glorious throne to welcome Stephen into heaven! I don't know how that hits you, but it thrills me! And the other thing we know as a result of this story which takes place in Chapter 7, is that in Chapter 9, the one holding the coats of those who threw the stones is moved to believe in Jesus too. I don't think the proximity of these events is any coincidence, I believe fully that it was Stephen's dying testimony that softened the heart of the Pharisee Saul and hastened the birth of the Apostle Paul!

V. What Can We Do?

With all of that being said, what is it that we can do today to stand together with our brothers and sisters who are being persecuted? One of the first things the Scripture tells us to do for the persecuted church is to remember them and to empathize with them. Hebrews 13:3 says, "Remember those in prison as if you were their fellow prisoners, and those who are mistreated as if you yourselves were suffering." And Paul tells us in 1 Cor. 12:26, *"If one part suffers, every part suffers with it; if one part is honored, every part rejoices with it."*

The next thing we are to do is to pray for them. *"Far be it from me that I should sin against the Lord by ceasing to pray for you,"* so says the prophet Samuel when asked to pray for the Israelites in trouble. We need to remember to pray for them daily, both specifically and generically.

Next we need to communicate with them and to affirm them in their faithfulness. That is the very example we learn from the Scriptures. We need to affirm their faithfulness to the church as Paul does in 1 Thess. 1:4 *"For we know, brothers loved by God, that he has chosen you."* We need to come alongside them and hold them up because of the injustice caused by their government. The writer of Proverbs tells us in 31:8 *"Speak up for those who cannot speak for themselves, for the rights of all who are destitute."* Isaiah empathizes with his people when he writes, *"Your country is desolate, your cities burned with fire; your fields are being stripped by foreigners right before you, laid waste as when overthrown by strangers."* And Listen to what Dr. James Dobson wrote recently, *"When I see something like this Christian persecution, my heart aches because the believers here don't even know about it, don't care. We're not expressing moral outrage; we're not indignant of the indifference of the United States government towards this. And we ought to be marching in the streets because our brethren are being persecuted, imprisoned, beaten, sold into slavery, and butchered and we don't seem to care in this country."*

We also need to actively support them. We can write to various government officials. We can form a coalition among churches to do more than we can do alone. We can contact organizations involved in ministering to the persecuted church and support them in prayer and in more practical ways as well. We also can go to them. We can participate in short-term missions trips; going to places where these things are happening, if God calls us to that kind of ministry. In Acts 16:9 Luke records the following: *"During the night Paul had a vision of a man of Macedonia standing and begging him, 'Come over to Macedonia and help us.'"* If you can't go to them then, where it's possible, write to them or email them, just as the Scripture demonstrates, *"To God's elect, strangers in the world, scattered throughout Pontus, Galatia, Cappadocia, Asia and Bithynia, who have been chosen according to the foreknowledge of God the Father, through the sanctifying work of the Spirit, for obedience to Jesus Christ and sprinkling by his blood. Grace and peace be yours in abundance."*

Finally, we can contribute financially toward our missions and remember that there are those around the world who are struggling with their very survival. Paul said it well in 2 Cor. 9:6-8. *"Remember this: Whoever sows sparingly will also reap sparingly, and whoever sows generously will also reap generously. Each man should give what he has decided in his heart to give, not reluctantly or under compulsion, for God loves a cheerful giver. And God is able to make all grace abound to you, so that in all things at all times, having all that you need, you will abound in every good work."*

IV. Conclusion

China, Shaanxi Province: *"The officers stripped three [Christian] brethren naked from the waist and forced the women to stand with them. The three men were beaten until they were totally covered with blood and had gaping wounds and injuries all over their bodies. As if such violent beating wasn't enough, the officers then hung them up and began to hit them with rods on their backs. They did this until the three men were unconscious and barely breathing."* The victims were Protestants. Their crime was communicating the love of Christ with foreigners.

Let me leave you with the words of martyred missionary Jim Elliott: *"He is no fool who gives up what he cannot keep to gain that which he cannot lose."*

Now, let's turn our attention back to that final church!

Chapter 9
"The Church of the Spittoon"

What God Is Saying to You as His Church

Revelation 3: 14-22

To the Church in Laodicea

[14]"To the angel of the church in Laodicea write:

These are the words of the Amen, the faithful and true witness, the ruler of God's creation. [15]I know your deeds, that you are neither cold nor hot. I wish you were either one or the other! [16]So, because you are lukewarm—neither hot nor cold—I am about to spit you out of my mouth. [17]You say, 'I am rich; I have acquired wealth and do not need a thing.' But you do not realize that you are wretched, pitiful, poor, blind and naked. [18]I counsel you to buy from me gold refined in the fire, so you can become rich; and white clothes to wear, so you can cover your shameful nakedness; and salve to put on your eyes, so you can see. [19]Those whom I love I rebuke and discipline. So be earnest, and repent. [20]Here I am! I stand at the door and knock. If anyone hears my voice and opens the door, I will come in and eat with him, and he with me. [21]To him who overcomes, I will give the right to sit with me on my throne, just as I overcame and sat down with my Father on his throne. [22]He who has an ear, let him hear what the Spirit says to the churches."

I. Introduction

We have finally reached the final piece of the puzzle on what Jesus is saying to each of us through the letters He sent to the churches of Asia Minor. I want to begin this final section by pointing out once again that the seven churches were seven literal churches.

This is important to remember as we interpret what is written, yet in hindsight of the scriptures it is easily seen that these churches have represented sections, times, or eras within the church age. I think that it would be valuable at this point in our discussion for me to point out precisely which eras of the church each one of these letters addresses. This is by no means an exact science, but it is interesting to ponder none the less. Let me make it clear that all of the letters have elements that apply to the church today, but it is equally applicable, through the lens of Church History, that they represent sections of the church age as well.

Ephesus was a church that had their first love wane. They needed a fresh love. They were the church that needed a second honeymoon. Everything they did was out of a sense of obligation. They had lost their fervor. In this church we see the Early Church, and at the end of the age leaven slipped in and corrupted their reasons for serving the Lord. This would be a picture of the first century church.

The second church to whom a letter was written was Smyrna. This was the church that needed courage because they were a persecuted church. Here is the picture of the second and third centuries, as the height of persecution against the church was prevalent.

Third, we see the church at Pergamos. This was a church, much like today, that had a problem with tolerating sin, hence my title for them, the church of tolerance. The compromising church was prevalent from 300 to about A.D. 500. The word pergamos means married, and during this age the church was married to the world. The doctrine of Balaam mentioned was the doctrine of tolerance. God has always hated the tolerance of sin.

The next church was Thyatira. This was the permissive Church since they allowed sinful leaders to pervert the church. The time frame from a historical perspective is longer now, it actually extends about a thousand years into the 1500's. This was the church during the Dark ages, a time that sin was prevalent. We come to the church in Sardis, the dead church. There was a remnant arising out of this time frame, but the church itself had died in their orthodoxy and rituals, and allowed the carnal world to infiltrate every fiber of the Church. This church time began in the 1500's and extended to about the early to mid 1700's. The Reformation was during this time. During this time the printing press began to make the Scriptures readily available. Every major language had a translation of the Scriptures for the very first time.

The result was a new era that grew from these humble beginnings, an era where the Word of God began to flourish and was used to form laws and nations. Revival began to sweep around the world. This is pictured by the church of Philadelphia, the only church of which God did not scold in some way. This began with the age of the awakening of world wide missions and evangelization. This is the time from the 1700's until now. But we can see the great day of the Philadelphian church is waning.

Now we come to Laodicea. This is the church about which God had nothing good to say. This is the last of the seven churches. The city of Laodicea was located about 40 miles southeast of Philadelphia. Approximately 35 years prior to this letter being written, the city had been destroyed by an earthquake, but, unlike Philadelphia, it was such a wealthy city that it had the ability to rebuild in a short time. They were famous for rich black wool, a medical school, and close by were the hot springs of Hieropolis and the cold water of Colossae. The water would meet in this city and be neither cold nor hot. We have no record that Paul ever went to Laodicea, but he was concerned for the church. In Colossians 2:1-2, he wrote, *"For I want you to know how much I am struggling for you, and for those in Laodicea, and for all who have not seen me face to face. I want their hearts to be encouraged and united in love, so that they may have all the riches assured understanding and have the knowledge of God's mystery, that is, Christ Himself.*" It is surprising how Jesus spoke to this church.

II. The Letter and Its Author

The great Judge now speaks as this letter to Laodicea is begun. He is the "Amen." This was a recognized Hebrew name of God! We find it used in Isaiah 65:16, that says, *"That he who blesses himself in the earth shall bless himself in the God of truth."* The word "truth" is the Hebrew word "Amam," from which we get our word "Amen." He declares his Deity repeatedly to this church, and here calls Himself the Truth. What a reflection of John 14:6, where Jesus declared He was the Truth.

He also is the faithful and true Witness, and so He will be in the Day of Judgment. By His Word and testimonies, a swift witness against all ungodly men will be heard. Mankind will stand without excuse before a holy God. Jesus then declares Himself to be the Originator of all, the beginning. This does not mean that He was the first creation of God, but the first cause of the creation. In the fact that Jesus is the creator reveals further His deity. It was Jehovah who created the world as we see in Psalms 33:6: *"By the word of the LORD (Jehovah) were the heavens made; and all the host of them by the breath of his mouth."* Then in Isaiah 45:12, we read, *"I have made the earth, and created man upon it: I, even my hands, have stretched out the heavens, and all their host have I commanded."* Verse 18 of the same chapter continues, *"For thus says the LORD (Jehovah again) that created the heavens; God (Elohiym) himself that formed the earth and made it; he has established it, he created it not in vain, he formed it to be inhabited: I am the LORD; and there is none else."*

It is clear that Jehovah is the self existent God that needs no other, the Creator of all. Thus it is evident and simple to believe that Jesus is Jehovah.

John 1:3 declares that *"All things were made by him; and without him was not any thing made that was made."* In Colossians we read,

"For by him were all things created, that are in heaven, and that are in earth, visible and invisible, whether they be thrones, or dominions, or principalities, or powers: all things were created by him, and for him: And he is before all things, and by him all things consist. " Jesus is the Beginning of all creation.

In Revelation 3:14, we find Jesus declaring His ownership of the church.

If you will take the time to look back at the other six churches, you will find a difference between our last one and the other six. Jesus addressed all other churches as either the "church of" or the "church in" their particular city. He did not address this one to the church in Laodicea, rather it was to the church of the Laodiceans. It was their church, not Christ's. The ownership of this body was themselves! It was a humanistic enterprise. This was an empty, religious group. They were a lost church.

In verses 15-17, we find the self-deception of this church. Jesus declares that He wished they were either cold or hot. They were not cold in their own eyes, they thought they were hot. A proper title for this section probably would be, *"When you think you're hot, but you're not. "* This church had an outer religion but no inner relationship. They had a profession without possession. They had empty professions made without faith, and were just as lost as before, yet they think they are rich! Jesus wanted them to be cold or hot so that they would recognize their needy position. They were not hot in God's eyes, they were deceived and floundering as lukewarm. God declared that He would spit them away. God would cast them away in the most repulsive way describable. This church literally made God nauseous. This church declared that they had it all, yet they were a lost church. Notice the words in verse 17 that Jesus uses to describe them. Though they said they were rich, Jesus said that they were *"wretched, and miserable, and poor, and blind, and naked."*

The word "wretched" means to be afflicted. It does not necessarily prove someone is without Christ, for Paul used it of himself in Romans 7:24, when he said, "O wretched man that I am!" He was referring to the battle within his flesh, so the wretched part was the affliction of the battle.

The next word that Jesus uses to describe this church is "miserable." This word means that they should be pitied. It is only used one other time in the Scriptures, and that is in 1 Corinthians 15:19. That verse says, *"If for this life only we have hoped in Christ, we are of all men most miserable."* The misery in this passage is descriptive of all of us if Jesus is not risen and we are yet in our sins, lost without Christ. So why would Jesus use this word to describe this lukewarm group of people? Why was this church to be pitied? Because they were living for this life alone!

Jesus then uses the word "poor" to describe this church. This church, in an earthly sense, lived in a very prosperous and wealthy city. In the beginning of this verse "they say that they are rich," so why would He say that they are poor? The word means to be destitute of wealth, influence, position and honor. It is translated 30 times as poor in our English Bible. At least once it is used to describe the "poor saints" in Macedonia. Once, James uses the word to describe a physically "poor man" that comes into the church in "vile raiment," and how the church should accept him. The other times it is translated as "beggar" speaking of Lazarus. All other times I can find, it is dealing with someone who is physically poor. But these were rich physically, so how were they poor? They were poor in the area that was most important, spiritually. None have to be poor spiritually. 2 Corinthians 8:9, speaking of what Christ did for those who will be saved, says, *"For you know the grace of our Lord Jesus Christ, that, though he was rich, yet for your sakes he became poor, that through his poverty you might be rich."* A saved person is not poor, and cannot be spiritually poor. Jesus has paid it all. We are made rich through His poverty.

The next word used is the word, "blind." In 2 Peter 1:9, it is used of saved people who have an impaired Spiritual vision. Any other time, we see that blindness is a picture of the lost.

The strongest adjective, in my opinion, is the last. Jesus announced that they were "naked," this means that they had no robe. The Robe of righteousness was not theirs. Think of the story Jesus told of the wedding in Matthew 22. In oriental weddings, a wedding garment was freely given by the host. For someone to enter, not being properly clothed, was an insult to the wedding. Jesus tells of one who was without a garment and was cast out. At the marriage supper of the Lamb, there will be none who do not have the garment of salvation. This church was naked, without a garment, without a robe. This is a picture of the carnal, lost church of the last days. This church does not belong to Christ. Religion is full of this type of people.

That they are a lost church makes the invitation of verses 18 and 21, even more clear. The great Counselor of heaven appeals to them to come and get what they need from Him. Gold so that they would not be poor and raiment so they would not be naked. He said they needed His "eye salve," so that they would not be blind. In Laodicea there was a famous medical school, and they were accustomed to treating themselves. God has said you need some spiritual eye salve to remove your blindness! He used terms that they clearly understood. He was not saying that they could buy salvation, but was using language similar to Isaiah 55:1, that says, *"Let every one that is thirst come to the water, and he that has no money; come, buy, and eat; yes, come, buy wine and milk without money and without price."*

In spite of their condition He was offering them everything. He was offering them Himself! To steal the words of the Mastercard commercial, what Jesus has for all that will come is "priceless." The price has been paid. It already has been tried by the fire, so they were invited to come and possess what Jesus had provided. They could now be rich, eyes opened, without pity, and clothed in righteousness.

In verses 20-22, we see an invitation to all as these notes from Jesus are coming to a close. This invitation is to all who have lived during the church age. The invitation is to come. When we preach, we are saying "come." When we witness, we are in harmony with Jesus and saying "come." Jesus said "come" in Matthew 11:28. He said, "Come unto me, all who labor and are heavy burdened, and I will give you rest." Verse 29 of that chapter speaks of the victorious Christian life, as one finds rest after they take the yoke of service upon themselves, but that is not the case in the verse that we have just seen. Any that come to Christ with the burden of sin, Jesus will freely give them rest. The invitation in Revelation 3 is a personal invitation. Jesus said that it was He who stands at this door. It is a beckoning call, for Jesus is knocking, beckoning others to be saved.

It is a universal call, anyone who opens the door will find salvation.

It is also a call of promise, for if anyone answers the call of Christ, they will find a relationship, fellowship, and citizenship.

III. Conclusion

This is precisely why Jesus dictated letters to His church before He revealed the coming judgment on the earth. The seven literal churches give us a glimpse of His church today, and more specifically, a glimpse of ourselves today. At the same time, we also see the prophecies of the church age coming to fulfillment. Oh that God's children will be faithful to look for the appearing of our Groom, our Lord and our King. May we possess the crown of which the Apostle Paul spoke, when he said in 2 Timothy 4:8, "*Henceforth there is laid up for me a crown of righteousness, which the Lord, the righteous judge, shall give me at that day: and not to me only, but unto all them also that love his appearing.*" And as we love the appearing of our Savior, may we say with the Apostle John, "*Even so, come, Lord Jesus.*"

As we come to the end of our exploration of the Word that God has for us in these letters to the Churches, we have learned a lot about what it means to be His Church, even now, in the 21st century. Now we need to look closer at God's instruction to His church in the first century so that we may know His truth for our lives today.

Becoming an
Acts 29
Believer

Chapter 10
"Becoming an Acts 29 Believer: An Introduction"

Acts 2: 42-47 & Acts 4: 32-37

The Fellowship of the Believers

[42]They devoted themselves to the apostles' teaching and to the fellowship, to the breaking of bread and to prayer. [43]Everyone was filled with awe, and many wonders and miraculous signs were done by the apostles. [44]All the believers were together and had everything in common. [45]Selling their possessions and goods, they gave to anyone as he had need. [46]Every day they continued to meet together in the temple courts. They broke bread in their homes and ate together with glad and sincere hearts, [47]praising God and enjoying the favor of all the people. And the Lord added to their number daily those who were being saved."

The Believers Share Their Possessions

[32]"All the believers were one in heart and mind. No one claimed that any of his possessions was his own, but they shared everything they had. [33]With great power the apostles continued to testify to the resurrection of the Lord Jesus, and much grace was upon them all. [34]There were no needy persons among them. For from time to time those who owned lands or houses sold them, brought the money from the sales [35]and put it at the apostles' feet, and it was distributed to anyone as he had need.

[36]Joseph, a Levite from Cyprus, whom the apostles called Barnabas (which means Son of Encouragement), [37]sold a field he owned and brought the money and put it at the apostles' feet.

I. Introduction

Our premise for this study is to advance the idea that God is speaking still today to His church and that the Scripture is a very clear instruction manual for the church. There is nothing new in that idea, however, to apply the concept to each one of us as individuals, maintaining the truth that each of us is "His church."

Every church has a chance to be the church God wants them to be. Every person can be the person God wants them to be. This has been discussed quite a bit in the last few years, the question is do we want to be believers who want to be all that God wants us to be? To be such a believer, in my opinion, means being willing to go back in time and learn what the First Century believers looked like, acted like, and felt like.

I used to hear from people all the time, even those who didn't go to church, what a nice church we had. It was true, we did have a nice church! But I wanted us to be more than just a "nice church. Actually I'm not so sure just how much of a compliment that is! "Nice churches" don't actually challenge anyone to do anything outside of their comfort zones. "Nice churches" don't actually offend anyone with the message of the truth. "Nice churches" do "nice" things for people and never engage in church discipline. I want to be part of more than just a nice church, I want to be part of the church I read about in the book of Acts where God was on the move. Don't you? Well, that same principle applies to us as individual believers. "Nice people" don't challenge anyone with the Truth. "Nice people" don't offend anyone with the message. Don't you want more than that? Don't you want to be a believer the way they were in the first days of the church? The early church has had a lot said and written about it, but I've never heard it referred to as a "nice church." As we move into this section of our work together, I would like for us to think of ourselves at the beginning of a new adventure. The following chapters are taken from a 7-week preaching series entitled: "Acts 29: Becoming The First Century Church!" that I shared with my church several years ago. In the following chapters, I want us to begin the process of examining ourselves and make the decision once and for all that we want to become believers who really make a major impact on our community and in the world for Jesus Christ! What do we want to look like and to be in the coming weeks, months and years as we seek to follow Jesus? Do we want to be so bold as to ask God what His dreams are for us as His Church? Or do we just want to keep going the way we are, doing good work, spending some time in Bible Study, but not really striving forward for all that God has for us? Can we just coast along as we are, probably for a while, but, as we've seen in our look at the letters to the Churches, we'd soon become useless to Him in reaching His dreams for us.

Is change coming to our lives as believers, you bet! Is it all good, probably not! Can it be good, absolutely! I do know one thing though, as long as God is God, change is inevitable. He is a God of change, He is a creative God always pushing us and stretching us and calling us to new and wonderful things!

In the previous chapters on the Letters to the Churches we see how He commands them, and then says if they don't respond He would take the candle stick from their midst, interesting none of these churches exist today. Why? They were disobedient to the Lord and refused to follow His lead, refused to ask Him to plant His dreams in them so that they could be a part of fulfilling them in the places they were planted.

I see God calling us to follow seven key elements in this process that if we do, He will bless us and use us to the full! I saw the members of my church heartily begin this process when they chose to embark upon the journey of creating a Mission Statement for the Church. Our

Mission statement was to: **"Follow Jesus Christ by knowing, growing, and showing His love and joy in a genuine way every day."** I believe, in my heart, that if each and every one of us were to truly adopt this mission for our individual lives we would become the believers that Jesus wants us to be.

However, in order to be able to do that, I do think there are five essential ingredients that we must include.

II. A Person of Prayer

The first thing is that God is calling us to be are People of Prayer. 2 Chronicles 7:14 says, *"if my people, who are called by my name, will humble themselves and pray and seek my face and turn from their wicked ways, then will I hear from heaven and will forgive their sin and will heal their land."*

Do we qualify for this promise? As believers in Jesus Christ, we are His people called by His name, but are we doing the rest? Toward that end I cannot encourage you enough to pray for and to participate in any Prayer Meeting that your church is offering. If your church does not have a prayer opportunity, find one somewhere else or start one. The Scripture reminds us that when "two or three are gathered together, there I am in the midst of them." I also encourage your participation in prayer on a regular basis every Sunday morning before and after your Worship gathering. You need to be praying for your own needs and for the needs of others, but also for seeking out what dreams God has for your Fellowship. Further, if you are not involved with a specific prayer partner, I encourage you to seek out someone you trust to share in prayer with on a very regular basis. You also need to continue to expand your prayer ministries as an individual and as a member of the local church of which you are a part.

Prayer is the foundation for all ministry and is the very capstone of the Christian life. How is your prayer life? Do you still just give God a shopping list and call it prayer? Do you really know all about prayer? I've been reading and studying about prayer for years and have just scratched the surface. Prayer is conversation with God, but it is so much more. And He is calling us to be a People of Prayer!

III. A Person of Mission
The second component is that God is calling you to become a People of Mission. Acts 1:8 says: "*But you will receive power when the Holy Spirit comes on you; and you will be my witnesses in Jerusalem, and in all Judea and Samaria, and to the ends of the earth.*" It is the business of the Church to be in missions. It is the business of every believer to be in missions. I am sure that the church where you attend supports missions through your weekly giving to the specific projects they have chosen to support, but are you attending a church that is truly *involved* in mission? I pray that the answer is "YES" for every church that is, I am forever grateful.

The church that Nancy & I pastored for 16 years was a church involved in missions. They not only supported the work of Child Evangelism, but they knew the local director and so many of them participated in its ministry in a number of other ways. They not only gave to the Good News Home, but they baked for their bake Sale and then went and bought back the food they had baked. They not only gave to the Market Street Mission, they invited them to the church for their graduation and so many of the members of the church fully participated in that great evening. They not only supported David & Judy Morton in the Middle East, but they invited David to the church regularly, and prayed for their family daily. They not only supported the people of Mississippi in their efforts to rebuild after Katrina, but they went there multiple times. They not only sent money to Haiti through their support of Dayspring Ministries, but they went there over and over again and fell in love with the people there! The people in that church grew in their missions outlook so very much, but is that enough? I really don't think we, as believers in Christ can ever do enough in this area.

Allow me to challenge you again to be in prayer about how God can use you to reach the world around you. Be in prayer and ask God to plant His dreams in you for reaching the world with the Good News of Jesus Christ. But also there's this: How can we reach others around us, missions is more than just doing for others, it is actually sharing Jesus so that others might know the joy we have found in Him! Missions are concerned with worldwide evangelism, but missions also is involved in personal evangelism, taking Christ to the world that begins in our own Jerusalem first! How many have we lead to Christ in recent weeks? Jesus told us He was sending the Holy Spirit to empower us to be His witnesses, if we're not, we need to examine ourselves and ask:

1) Am I truly saved…have I given my life to Christ?

2) Do I really have the power of the Holy Spirit in my life so I will effect the lives of others?

3) Am I just refusing to answer the call on my life that Christ has placed on us?

Let's be in prayer as to how God wants to lead us in missions to the world around us, beginning in Jerusalem, moving on to Judea, Samaria, and truly to the ends of the earth. What is God's dream for us in the area of missions and evangelism in our lives? Why don't we just ask Him?

IV. A Person of Purpose

Third, God is calling us to become People of Purpose. If I were to give a quiz today on what the purpose of the church is, how many of us would pass? So much of what we think the church is here for is wrong. A poll was taken a couple of years ago and the standard answer was that the church was here to serve its members. WRONG! The church is here to serve those who aren't yet members! The church is not a club, it is a place where we are trained to do service in the world. It's not a question of what can the church do for me, it's "What can I do for others?" Paraphrasing John Kennedy's great line:

"Ask not what the church can do for you, but what you can do for the Church!" The purpose of the church is "To Reach, To Win, To Train, and To Send." That's what "knowing, growing, and showing" is all about! Where do you fit in all that? And I mean, "in ALL of it? No one is exempt, everyone who believes in Jesus Christ is called! There are so many needs in our communities that we can meet, but we're not, because we are not stepping up to meet them! We need someone willing to reach out to the young people of our communities in a way that will actually engage them. We need to be people who are willing to actually go and be in the school system and be willing to be Jesus with skin on in that arena. We need to be people who participate in meeting the physical needs of people in our communities who are falling through the cracks. We need to be people who will reach out to our Senior Citizens and provide for their needs and help them become more active and vital in our communities. The list goes on and on, there is a never ending list of what we could be doing to answer the call of God as His Church. We need to ask Him to plant His dreams in us for our purpose here in whatever vineyard He has planted us in.

V. A Person of Growth

Fourth, God is calling us to be People of Growth. Growth in terms of sharing the Good News and helping others come to a saving knowledge of Jesus Christ and growth in terms of the depth and breadth of our own walk with Jesus. Later on, Chapter 14 will deal more specifically with the concept of our growth as His people.

VI. A Person of Learning

The next thing that I notice in the First Century church that God is calling us to see is that we need to be people of Learning. We need to be believers committed to being in His Word on a regular basis, both corporately and personally. I had a dream a number of years ago that God had placed on my heart and I have not seen it come to fruition, but I still believe it is His dream that 100% of believers would be involved in the study of His Word. Toward that end, most of our churches offer studies in which we can participate and many other ministries do as well. There is no excuse for not finding a Bible Study in which you can be a part. If you are not studying the Word, God wants you to study the Word. If you are not in a study with other believers, God wants you to be so that, in the words of Proverbs 27:17, "iron can sharpen iron!" If you do not have a personal daily reading plan for the Scripture, God wants you to develop one and commit yourself to it. In Acts 17 we read about the blessing at Berea and how the sole origin of that blessing was the receiving the Word, the readiness to follow the Word, and the daily study of the Word. We need to be a Person of Learning!

VII. A Person of Worship

In our effort to emulate the example of the First Century Church, we need to become a People of Worship. In the words of that great praise song, we need to come back to the heart of worship. We need to praise our God in everything that we say, everything that we do, everything that we think. We need to sing our praises to God in psalms, hymns, and spiritual songs. We need to be writing new poems, writing new songs, sharing new testimonies, using whatever gifts He has given us to bring glory and honor and blessing to His Holy Name! We need to sing our praises to God in reading aloud and listening to the blessing of His Word. We need to sing our praises to God through our mutual service one to another. We need to sing our praises to God through an ever growing desire to spend time with Him and grow closer to Him. We need to be a People of Worship!

VII. A Person of Vision

Finally, God is calling us to be a People of Vision. Proverbs 29:18 says, "*Where there is no vision, the people perish.*" I know this can be very dangerous, people with vision are always struggling. People with vision are sometimes hard to live with, but are necessary if we are to follow God's leading. George Bernard Shaw and Robert Kennedy were both famous for saying, "*Some people see things as they are and ask why, I dream thing that never were and ask why not?*" We need to be visionaries that will pray and wait on Him to see what the vision God has in mind for us as His church. Some big ideas are there just waiting for the right people to come and bring them to life.

I have a vision of ministries led by people of vision and with the gifts and graces to carry them out. I am convinced that this vision is precisely what it means to be His church. I am convinced, based on the Scripture, that God is calling us to be: **A person of prayer; a person of mission; a person of purpose; a person of growth; a person of learning; a person of worship; and a person of vision.**

Will you join me in asking God's dreams for you as His church to look expectantly forward to all that He has in store for you? It is my dream that as you read the following chapters God will reveal to you how to better be a person of prayer, mission, purpose, growth, learning, worship, and vision.

The next seven chapters will be a deeper explanation of each of those areas, and I encourage you to focus your attention, your prayers, and your efforts! May God bless you in this quest.

Chapter 11
"Becoming an Acts 29 Believer: A Person of Prayer"

2 Chronicles 7: 1-14

The Dedication of the Temple

[1]"When Solomon finished praying, fire came down from heaven and consumed the burnt offering and the sacrifices, and the glory of the LORD filled the temple. [2] The priests could not enter the temple of the LORD because the glory of the LORD filled it. [3] When all the Israelites saw the fire coming down and the glory of the LORD above the temple, they knelt on the pavement with their faces to the ground, and they worshiped and gave thanks to the LORD, saying, 'He is good; his love endures forever.'

[4] Then the king and all the people offered sacrifices before the LORD. [5]And King Solomon offered a sacrifice of twenty-two thousand head of cattle and a hundred and twenty thousand sheep and goats. So the king and all the people dedicated the temple of God. [6] The priests took their positions, as did the Levites with the LORD's musical instruments, which King David had made for praising the LORD and which were used when he gave thanks, saying, "His love endures forever." Opposite the Levites, the priests blew their trumpets, and all the Israelites were standing.

[7] Solomon consecrated the middle part of the courtyard in front of the temple of the LORD, and there he offered burnt offerings and the fat of the fellowship offerings, [a] because the bronze altar he had made

could not hold the burnt offerings, the grain offerings and the fat portions.

[8] So Solomon observed the festival at that time for seven days, and all Israel with him—a vast assembly, people from Lebo [b] Hamath to the Wadi of Egypt. [9] On the eighth day they held an assembly, for they had celebrated the dedication of the altar for seven days and the festival for seven days more. [10] On the twenty-third day of the seventh month he sent the people to their homes, joyful and glad in heart for the good things the LORD had done for David and Solomon and for his people Israel.

The LORD Appears to Solomon

[11] When Solomon had finished the temple of the LORD and the royal palace, and had succeeded in carrying out all he had in mind to do in the temple of the LORD and in his own palace, [12] the LORD appeared to him at night and said: "I have heard your prayer and have chosen this place for myself as a temple for sacrifices.

[13] "When I shut up the heavens so that there is no rain, or command locusts to devour the land or send a plague among my people, [14] if my people, who are called by my name, will humble themselves and pray and seek my face and turn from their wicked ways, then will I hear from heaven and will forgive their sin and will heal their land."

I. Introduction

In the last chapter we introduced the concept of becoming an Acts 29 believer and outlined a number of arenas in which we must move to achieve this end. We talked about 7 things are that necessary for us to follow the lead of our predecessors in the early church 20 centuries ago. We talked about the need to become a Person of Mission, a Person of Purpose, a Person of Growth, a Person of Learning, a Person of Worship, a Person of Vision, and the topic for this chapter, "Becoming a Person of Prayer!"

Over my years as a pastor, I talked a lot about allowing God to plant

His dreams in us and for us, to allow them to grow into fulfillment through us. It is my contention that one of God's dreams for us is to meet the single greatest need in our community today. Sounds like a tall order right out of the box, but I am sure that it's true. The single greatest need in our community today is a true Heaven-sent revival! And this is something we can not do ourselves. Programs don't do it, preaching can't do it, Bible Study can't do it, the type music we use in our churches can't do it! Only God, moving by His Holy Spirit can do it! It will be because a sovereign God intervened in the lives of His people that our Worship will take on a whole new life. It will be because an all-powerful, all-knowing, loving Lord got a hold of His people that our praise and our prayers and our service will come to life. It will be because God decided it was His time to do so that our outreach efforts will finally pay off in the reaching of the lost for Christ!

Real revival is God's idea and it is God initiative and it is God's doing! Real revival is not built on emotions and sentimental thoughts or even eyes full to tears, this can all be brought up by emotionalism. The word "revival" means to "live again," it is God's people coming alive again to our responsibilities toward our Creator, it is God's people returning to a life again.

II. Recipe for Revival

There is a recipe for revival in the Bible, which is found in text with which we began this chapter, 2 Chronicles 7. This is part of Solomon's dedication of the New Temple he has just completed for God.

In the Chapter 6 there is Solomon's prayer of dedication When you read this prayer you'll notice it has nothing to do with the temple, nothing to do with the building itself, instead, it had everything to do with the people of God who would come and pray in this Temple!

Solomon knew that that the God of Israel could not be contained in a building. Solomon, in his great wisdom, knew something we have come to know centuries later, that God is far more interested in residing in the hearts of His people than in some building made with hands!

In 1 Corinthians 6:19-20, Paul writes, *"Do you not know that your body is a temple of the Holy Spirit, who is in you, whom you have received from God? You are not your own; you were bought at a price. Therefore honor God with your body."*

Solomon knew that if revival was to come to the people of God that they would have to come to understand this truth and begin to act like it! With that being said, the question before us in our quest to become an Acts 29 believer is this:

III. How Will We Know When Revival Comes?

How will we know when revival comes into our lives? First, we will begin to see the fire fall! 2 Chronicles 7:1 says, *"When Solomon finished praying, fire came down from heaven and consumed the burnt offering and the sacrifices, and the glory of the LORD filled the temple."* So what does that have to do with us, 3000 years later? We are told by the Word that as the people of God we are to offer our bodies as living sacrifices to God. Romans 12:1-2, *"Therefore, I urge you, brothers, in view of God's mercy, to offer your bodies as living sacrifices, holy and pleasing to God—this is your spiritual act of worship. Do not conform any longer to the pattern of this world, but be transformed by the renewing of your mind. Then you will be able to test and approve what God's will is—his good, pleasing and perfect will."*

On the day of Pentecost, the fire fell from Heaven, not on the animals in the Temple, but instead fire fell on the believers themselves! When God, through His Holy Spirit descends on us with an outpouring of His grace, we to will see His fire fall. This is something only God can do! Nobody is interested in empty religion!

Nobody is clamoring for dull singing! Nobody is getting saved by dead praying! We need to give up trying to be religious and start living like we're on fire! We need to look for the real thing, for God's fire to fall on us again! A long time ago, in my first apartment, I converted an unused attic into a family room, and it was really a cool room. The only thing it was missing was a fireplace! So I built one, sort of. I glued some Z-Brick to the front of a piece of plywood, created a little fireplace setting, bought one of those Velcro fake fireplace things and presto, I had a fireplace! The only problem was, it wasn't real; it had no real flames, it gave off no real heat, and worst of all, it looked fake! To this day my wife, Nancy, laughs at me whenever we think about that creation of mine, a fake fireplace? Well, that's what empty religion is like; fake, no flames, no real heat, and worst of all, it looks fake! We need the real heat that comes from the fire of God that consumes the sacrifice with the understanding that WE ARE THE SACRIFICE!

Are you being consumed by God's fire? Are you being consumed by God's Anointing? You, as a believer in Jesus Christ, are the light of the world pointing others to Him. Without God's fire, without God's light, you can not do very much shining!

IV. The Glory of the Lord
When Revival comes we will witness the GLORY OF THE LORD.

2Chronicles 7:2, *"The priests could not enter the temple of the LORD because the glory of the LORD filled it."* This wasn't the first time this had happened in the history of God's people. At other times the Shekinah Glory of God came down like this, and when it happens, everything else takes a back seat. What we once thought so important is not important at all! Our focus will instead be where it always ought to be, on the glory of the Lord, on the Son, Jesus Christ! Eyes won't be on the preacher! Attention won't be on the music! Everything else will pale in comparison to the overwhelming sense of the presence of the Lord! And worship will be our first priority.

2 Chronicles 7:3, *"When all the Israelites saw the fire coming down and the glory of the LORD above the temple, they knelt on*

the pavement with their faces to the ground, and they worshiped and gave thanks to the LORD, saying, He is good; his love endures forever." 2 Chronicles 7:6, "*The priests took their positions, as did the Levites with the LORD's musical instruments, which King David had made for praising the LORD and which were used when he gave thanks, saying, 'His love endures forever.' Opposite the Levites, the priests blew their trumpets, and all the Israelites were standing.*"

Praising God will take the place of much of what is currently at the center of our lives. My family tries to go to worship at a great Christian retreat center called, Blue Mountain as often as we can get away. One of the reasons we enjoy it so much is the worship and praise time are so alive. When the Spirit of God is moving so richly in a Celebration of Worship that He is tangible, then worship is easy. The singing has sometimes been well over an hour and it feels like just a few minutes have come and gone! Why is it that our hearts aren't always in worship like they ought to be? Why is the freedom and spontaneity and joy we read about in the First Century believers so missing in the praise & worship of the people of our time? Is it still available to us today? In a simple word, "yes!" It is still available to us today, if only we will allow God to move in us and through us! And the form isn't what's important, it's our hearts tuned to God that make all the difference! I've experienced God's move in a high-Church Catholic Mass and in a store-front Pentecostal Church. It is possible anywhere where God is truly worshipped, where the worshippers offer themselves as living sacrifices!

Another thing that always happens when God is so present is that the giving is phenomenal! The priest in the temple offered up 22,000 oxen, 120,000 sheep! Where do you think all of those animals came from? They came from the people of God! And you also will see more and more folks coming to worship, more and more folks praising and serving the Risen Lord! Jesus said in John 12:32, "*But I, when I am lifted up from the earth, will draw all men unto Me!*"

V. How Does It Happen?

The big question for us in our attempt to become Acts 29 Believers is this: How does it happen? Revival doesn't come cheaply, it only comes when God's people pray! That's why it is so critical for us to become a Person of Prayer! It is essential that the people of God unite in prayer. It wasn't until after the prayer of the people that the fire fell! The early church experienced revival because the people were constantly in prayer! We need to pray daily in our own quiet spaces. We need to come together to pray which is why a weekly Prayer Meeting and Prayer Breakfast are so important! Prayer is not an option, prayer is an essential element to being an Acts 29 Believer! We have a responsibility to be in prayer and we receive such an incredible blessing from being in prayer. God said it best when He spoke to Jeremiah and said, *"Call to me and I will answer you and tell you great and unsearchable things you do not know."*

We learn from Solomon and we learn from the early believers that our prayers need to be coupled with humility. There was nothing magical about Solomon's prayer, it was just a prayer offered in humility! We must come before God humbly, James writes, *"Humble yourselves before the Lord, and he will lift you up."*

We also learn that our prayer needs to be coupled, not only with humility, but also with seeking God's face! To seek God's face means we must abandon all self-seeking. When we pray, we must not pray to get God on our side, He's already on our side as believers in Him, but rather we must pray to get in line with God's will. We pray to let go of our own stuff in the interest of taking on God's stuff! We pray so that we can let go of our own dreams in the exciting prospect of receiving God's dreams in their place!

We also learn that our prayer needs to be coupled with a true, heart-felt repentance! Sin blocks our prayers. The trash has to be hauled out of our lives so God can hear us. How exciting it is to know that the Creator of the universe wants to talk directly to us, and will, just as soon as we remove the obstacles to hearing Him speak!

VI. What Are the Results of Revival?

We learn from this passage and we know from watching the members of the First Century church, that when we "humble ourselves and pray and seek His face and turn from our wicked ways, that He will hear us! When the conditions are met God will hear from heaven!

Every great revival in the history of the Church has begun with prayer! Prayer truly changes the world! When we get serious about prayer, revival will not be far behind. I started this part of our work with Prayer because it is the cornerstone to everything else that we do. We cannot be a people of Mission, Purpose, Growth, Learning, Worship or Vision without first being a Person of Prayer. When we pray, truly pray, God will hear our prayers!

Also, when we pray, God will forgive us! When God brings revival we will be more sensitive to sin in our lives. We will see more folks come to Jesus as they experience this forgiveness and see it in our lives. There will be an atmosphere of forgiveness rather than condemning and fault finding. The power of forgiveness will just explode and saturate the whole landscape. And that is what is so exciting and so attractive to a world seeking answers to their most pressing questions, when they seek God in a genuine way, they will recognize their own sin and confess it and they will be forgiven!

Further, God will heal our land! We normally think of healing as being physical and that is certainly part of His promises to us. But here, God is saying He will heal our land, He will heal our churches, He will heal our marriages, He will heal the brokenhearted, He will heal the sin sick soul. When revival comes to a believer's heart it doesn't stop there! It goes home with you, it goes to church with you, it goes to school with you, it goes to the office with you, it goes to your business with you, it goes to your social gatherings with you, it goes to the Little League field with you. God promises to bring healing!

VI. Conclusion

To become an Acts 29 believer, we need to become a Person of Prayer. We need to become a Person of Prayer because it will only be in so doing that we will be in a position to assist God in meeting the greatest need in our land today, the greatest need in our churches today, the greatest need in our lives today. The need for a Holy Spirit Revival! May God help us to earnestly and fervently pray, to humble ourselves, to seek God's face, to turn from our wicked ways. May God help us to become a Person of Prayer on our way toward receiving from Him the revival He wants to bring!

Chapter 12
"Becoming a Acts 29 Believer: A Person of Mission"

Acts 13:1-3

Barnabas and Saul Sent Off

"¹In the church at Antioch there were prophets and teachers: Barnabas, Simeon called Niger, Lucius of Cyrene, Manaen (who had been brought up with Herod the tetrarch) and Saul. ²While they were worshiping the Lord and fasting, the Holy Spirit said, "Set apart for me Barnabas and Saul for the work to which I have called them." ³So after they had fasted and prayed, they placed their hands on them and sent them off."

I. Introduction

In the previous two chapters we've been looking at how we can become an Acts 29 believer, a believer modeled on the exciting times and people of the First Century Church! We want to learn how we can move from being a "nice" person, to being a person that makes a difference? In the introduction to this section of work, I shared that I had heard people in our community talk about our church as a "nice" church. Can you imagine the church in Jerusalem being called "a nice church?" Absolutely not! They were about the business of effectively changing their world for Jesus Christ! And because they were in that business, the "Redemption Business," they were forever causing conflict with the powers-that-be in their world. They were causing problems in their own families. They were causing problems in the market place. They were causing problems in their social settings. They were causing problems everywhere! They were turning their world upside down for Jesus! And this is still the role of believers in the world today; to challenge, to call people to follow Jesus and change from their "wicked ways!"

In the last chapter, we saw that we are to be a Person of Prayer, in order to bring revival, radical, life changing, Holy Spirit-led revival. The kind of revival that changes lives. The kind of revival that changes communities. The kind of revival that changes the world! Along with Prayer, another thing God is calling us to in order to be an Acts 29 Person is MISSION.

II. A Mission-Minded Believer

A believer that is not mission minded is by definition not a believer! That person is a person who makes little or no impact on the world. When you read the book of Acts we see believers of action and people who were concerned with the spread of the Word of God and Gospel of Jesus Christ. This is one of the keys that made them effective. This is why they made so many lives miserable. This is why they turned the world upside down.

We read in our Scripture text at the outset of this chapter, a portion from Acts when the Church at Antioch sent Paul and Barnabas out, launching Paul's first missionary journey. We need to notice two things about these believers: First, in verse 1 we see that the people of the church were working under the leadership of the Holy Spirit, "they had *prophets and teachers.*" Second, in verse 2 we see that they were "*worshiping the Lord and fasting,*" seeking God's will for their lives.

They were actually seeking to find out what God had in store for them. They were earnestly asking the Lord to plant His dreams in them for this fledgling experience that was the early church! I think that too many times, we do things the opposite way of our First Century forefathers; we make a decision, we make plans, and then we ask God to bless those plans! Here they are in Antioch, seeking God's will for their daily lives, seeking God's dreams for them as His agents in this world. Verse 2 says, *"While they were worshiping the Lord and fasting, the Holy Spirit said, "Set apart for me Barnabas and Saul for the work to which I have called them."* This time spent praying, worshiping and fasting actually launched the Church into the world!

We also see in 1 Corinthians 16: 5-9, Paul writing to the Corinthian Church about his third missionary journey into the world with these words, *"After I go through Macedonia, I will come to you—for I will be going through Macedonia. Perhaps I will stay with you awhile, or even spend the winter, so that you can help me on my journey, wherever I go. I do not want to see you now and make only a passing visit; I hope to spend some time with you, if the Lord permits. But I will stay on at Ephesus until Pentecost, because a great door for effective work has opened to me, and there are many who oppose me.*

Do you hear what Paul is saying here? He's tired, he's been on 2 other missionary journeys with no break; he's been preaching, starting churches, facing opposition, sometimes even having to flee from those wanting to kill him. He's hoping to take that break and come to Corinth to rest for a while, however, notice what he says *"a great door for effective work has opened to me ... "* What happens next is that Paul stays in Ephesus for another 3 years, the longest he was anywhere! Not only did God use Paul to start a great church in Ephesus, but while he was there many more churches were started all over the world. Ephesus became one of the major Christian Centers of the early church. And all because the people were praying for God's dreams to become their dreams, all because Paul earnestly sought the Lord's will and not his own, all because the people in the First Century Church were a "missions-minded" people!

Here's the point I want to make: When Paul saw the great Door of Opportunity, he saw it also as a Door of Obligation and a Door of Opposition.

III. A Door of Opportunity

Ephesus was not where most Christians would want to settle. It was a big city, a major financial and commercial center and a rich city, but it was also the home to the Temple of Diana, architecturally one of the seven wonders of the ancient world. However, this was a place of great immorality, a place filled with vice, corruption, and idol worship, a place where prostitution was actually used as a form of worship! It was a city full of superstitious people. But when Paul saw the City and saw all of the thousands of people who lived there, he saw a magnificent opportunity to spread the Gospel!

The difference between a pessimist and an optimist is that a pessimist sees a problem in every opportunity and an optimist sees an opportunity in every problem. Do you have a door of opportunity where you are? YOU BET YOU DO!!!! Living in America, you are living in the modern-day equivalent of Ephesus and you have an opportunity to touch so many more people with the Gospel of Jesus than anywhere else on earth, at any other time since Christ's resurrection! We are living in a land that is given over to vice, corruption, and idol worship in precisely the same way that Ephesus was 2000 years ago. We are living right in the middle of the most resources, financial and human, that the world has ever seen in one geographic location in its history! There are more people, more money, and more potential in 21st century America than anywhere else in the world! Furthermore, in spite of our sophistication, in spite of our exposure to the Gospel, we are rapidly becoming one of the least evangelized populations in the entire world! Imagine how many unsaved people are within a one hour drive of our homes and all that potential for the Kingdom of God! We don't even have to go anywhere else, they are right here in our own backyard! God is giving us a chance to seize the moment to catch the vision of what can be, are you ready to do it?

IV. A Door of Obligation

As Paul set out for Ephesus, not only did he see a Door of Opportunity, but he also recognized that this was a door of obligation. We have an obligation as believers to take the Gospel of Christ to others. What did Jesus say before ascending into Heaven in the first chapter of the Book of Acts: He said, *"But you will receive power when the Holy Spirit comes on you; and YOU WILL BE my witnesses in Jerusalem, and in all Judea and Samaria, and to the ends of the earth."* Notice He said, "YOU WILL BE!"

Do you feel that sense of obligation? We've got to realize that I can't do the work for you and that you can't do my work for me. Paul didn't say here that the door had opened for Barnabas and Timothy.

He felt the obligation to stay and do the work because he felt the call on his life from God Himself. God is forever opening doors, but it is our responsibility to go through them when He does! God is forever providing doors of opportunity, as His faithful followers, we have got to recognize those doors as doors of obligation for us! Perhaps the sound of the word *"obligation"* doesn't sound so good to you. Then maybe we should put the question this way, *"Do we allow our hearts to be broken by the things that break God's heart?"* *"Do we really care what happens to the people God has given us the awesome opportunity to minister to?"* Sometimes I think we shy away from the words "obligation" or "responsibility" because we think it sounds too much like "we have to do something" rather than "we want to do something." I love that sentiment, but just because we want to do something doesn't make it any less of a responsibility to be done; and the truth is we don't always WANT to do what God calls us to do. So often we might find ourselves praying: *"Father, if this cup can pass from me, let it!"* But even when that occurs, we need to keep on praying, *"But, nevertheless, Your will be done, but mine!"*

119

V. There Is Also the Door of Opposition

One last thing, whenever God moves there always are people who want to oppose Him, many not even realizing that is what they are doing. In Ephesus, it was open opposition from the worshippers and business men who made their living off the worship of Diana. But perhaps the worst opponents of the Gospel are not its enemies, but rather the nominal believers who heard the message, see people who are lost, but do nothing to make a difference! What are you doing to make a real difference in your church, your community, your place of business, in your schools? God is opening all kinds of doors for all of us right now, but there will undoubtedly be opponents. We cannot afford to look at the potential problems, instead we have got to seize the opportunities! The old adage goes something like this: "*If you are not a part of the solution, then you are a part of the problem!*" If we are honest with ourselves, then we know exactly on which side of that equation we stand, we know if we are a part of the solution and we know if we are a part of the problem!

In spite of the potential for opposition, in spite of the difficulties that lie ahead, in spite of the odds stacked up against us, we MUST become a Person of Mission! We must become people who reach out beyond the four walls of our churches to a world that so desperately needs to hear the Good News of Jesus Christ. Remember what Jesus said: "*But you WILL receive power when the Holy Spirit comes on you; and you WILL BE my witnesses in Jerusalem, and in all of Judea and Samaria, and to the ends of the earth.*"

Let us be a Person of Missions in our Jerusalems, in our homes, sharing the Good News with our husbands and our wives, our children and our parents, our brothers and our sisters. Let us be a Person of Missions in our Judeas, sharing the Good News at work, at school, in our social settings, on the ball fields, in the grocery stores! Let us be a Person of Missions in our Samaria, sharing the Good News through the people living on the streets, to the people suffering with addictions, to the people in prisons. Sharing the Good News to the people of

America, people with more resources and more potential for the Kingdom than any concentrated area in the history of the world. Let us be a Person of Missions to the ends of the earth, continuing to share the Good News in Haiti, in the Middle East, in China, India and Central America, in Uganda and the aids-ridden countries of Africa, and in countless other ways the Lord might place on your heart. Remembering that being a Person of Mission involves our giving to be sure, but it involves so much more than just our giving. It requires our involvement, it requires our obedience, it requires our willingness to be on the front-lines of missions in the world, whether they be in Jordan or Port-Au-Prince or Chicago or New York City! Are you ready should God call you today to move to whatever mission field He has in store for you? Are you ready should God say in the sound of your hearing: "Who will go for us, whom shall I send?" Are you ready to say: "Here I am, Lord, send me!" Are you ready?

Lord, lead us to be as You designed us to be, a true Person of Missions in the 21st century!

Chapter 13
"Becoming an Acts 29 Believer: A Person of Purpose

2 Corinthians 5:1-7

Our Heavenly Dwelling
"¹Now we know that if the earthly tent we live in is destroyed, we have a building from God, an eternal house in heaven, not built by human hands. ²Meanwhile we groan, longing to be clothed with our heavenly dwelling, ³because when we are clothed, we will not be found naked. ⁴For while we are in this tent, we groan and are burdened, because we do not wish to be unclothed but to be clothed with our heavenly dwelling, so that what is mortal may be swallowed up by life. ⁵Now it is God who has made us for this very purpose and has given us the Spirit as a deposit, guaranteeing what is to come.

⁶Therefore we are always confident and know that as long as we are at home in the body we are away from the Lord. ⁷We live by faith, not by sight."

I. Introduction
As we continue our look at being an Acts 29 believer, becoming a Person of Prayer and becoming a Person of Missions, now we turn our attention to becoming a Person of Purpose! Proverbs 19:21 says, *"Many are the plans in a man's heart, but it is the Lord's purpose that prevails."* I really like this proverb, especially in light of the truth that no matter what we might plan in our hearts and minds, no matter

how good or evil it may be, God's purpose ultimately, will always prevail! So the big question is this: "What is God's purpose?" The answer to that critical question is all wrapped up in what He purposes for His followers. And this is no passing fancy, no intellectual pursuit for the challenge of it, it is what Jesus came and gave His life for! Jesus came to earth, lived His life and died a terrible death so that God's purpose could be achieved!

The key truth that we have got to understand about the church is this: the church is not a religious club; it's not a service organization; it's not a business; and, it's not a building! The church is an organism, it is a living, breathing organism; the church is the Body of Christ! More specifically, the church is you as a follower of Christ! Paul writes in 1 Corinthians 12:27: "*Now you are the body of Christ, and each one of you is a part of it.*" God didn't just establish the church and then leave it on its own! Instead, He has given you a purpose!

We could spend days on trying to flesh this all out, many have spent years writing books on the subject, but, for our purposes I want to make it as simple and straight forward as possible. Jesus stated the purpose when He said as He was about to leave His disciples to ascend into heaven. "*All authority in heaven and on earth has been given to me. Therefore go and make disciples of all nations, baptizing them in the name of the Father and of the Son and of the Holy Spirit, and teaching them to obey everything I have commanded you. And surely I am with you always, to the very end of the age.*" This instruction from the Lord has been called "The Great Commission, "the marching orders for the Church," which are really YOUR individual marching orders, and as such, everything we do should be derived from this call of God on our lives as the Church of Jesus Christ, as His Body in this world. And let me repeat this again, YOU are the Church of Jesus Christ!

It all boils down to four things: the purpose of every believer is to reach, to win, to train, and to send!

II. To Reach

Everything Jesus did while He walked on the earth was carefully designed to reach out to lost people who needed Him so desperately. Yes, there were times He went off by Himself and spent time with His 12 closest followers. But even when He did, it was designed to teach, train, and prepare them for reaching out to others. A tremendous percentage of His recorded earthly ministry was aimed at reaching the common folk of His day! His last words on earth before ascending into Heaven were instruction to us to reach out to those around us. Whether you turn to the end of the Gospel of Matthew and hear Jesus say: *"Therefore go and make disciples of all nations, baptizing them in the name of the Father and of the Son and of the Holy Spirit, and teaching them to obey everything I have commanded you."* Or whether you turn to Luke's account in the beginning of the Book of Acts where Jesus says: *"But you will receive power when the Holy Spirit comes on you; and you will be my witnesses in Jerusalem, and in all Judea and Samaria, and to the ends of the earth."* We get the picture. The most important thing that Jesus wanted us to know before He left and went to Heaven was this: "REACH OUT to a lost and dying world with the Good News of the Gospel!"

Paul recognized that fact and lived it out in his own life and wrote about it throughout his letters to the churches. three out of the five ministry gifts he discusses in Ephesians 4 deal directly with reaching out. Ephesians 4:11 reads: *"It was He who gave some to be apostles, some to be prophets, some to be evangelists, and some to be pastors and teachers ... "* It's only the pastors and teachers who focus on the ones in the church already, and even there, the pastors and teachers are designed to prepare the others to reach out in the name of Christ! Anyway that you study the Scripture, you must come away with the same conclusion, the essential job of the believer, our essential job as a believer today, is to look for ways to reach out with the love of God to our community and to the world! That is our reason for being! That is our purpose!

III. To Win

As critical as it is, it is not enough just to reach people, we also have to win them to Christ. Unfortunately, through the ages, being saved and being part of a church are not always the same thing.

Salvation comes as we commit ourselves to Christ and His ministry here on earth. Commitment and membership are not always the same thing. Commitment is not a casual thing! An analogy can be made to a marriage, just as marriage is more than a wedding ceremony, so being committed to Jesus Christ is more than simply joining a church. Imagine how long a marriage would last if most of us did in our marriages what we do when we join a church? In fact, we don't have to imagine, all we need to do is look around and see what happens when we fail to make that commitment to marriage. The same is true with our marriage to Jesus! Just as a marriage takes commitment, time, effort, work, learning to live with one another, and intimacy, so does our commitment to the Body of Christ! To say that it is part of our purpose to "win people to Christ" means that it is our role to help lead people into a more intimate relationship with God through Jesus Christ in the power of the Holy Spirit! Remembering always that it is the Spirit's job to do the work of salvation, it is merely our job to allow others to see the overwhelming benefits of that relationship by living it out in our own lives!

If you have ever wondered what marks the difference between a moving, growing, exciting, believer and an average, run of the mill, every street corner kind of church-goer, it's this: It is in direct proportion to the commitment of the individual to the work of Christ in the world. They are not only the ones who have reached out to the world with the Gospel, but they also are the ones who live out the joy of that relationship! Won over by the love of the Lord, they are fully committed to sharing the joy of that relationship with everyone who they meet! They become those who simply cannot help being a walking, talking, billboard for Jesus. They become those whose lives have been radically changed by the power and presence of Jesus in them. They become those who can't get enough of Jesus themselves! They become those who continue to grow and prosper in their walk with their Lord!

IV. To Train

In Matthew 28:19, Jesus says: *"Therefore go and make disciples..."* The purpose of believers is to Reach the lost and to Win them for Christ, but it is also to make disciples! When Jesus spoke those words, He wasn't speaking to an organization. He was speaking to His disciples as individual followers of His. It is relatively easy to become a church member, in fact it's actually harder to become a member of a country club than it is to become a member of most churches. I sometimes wonder if we don't make it too easy, does it become too cheap somehow? Christ gave His life for the Church, what are we going to give in return? The basic call of Jesus is for us to become His disciples! A disciple is someone who learns from the Master and puts into practice what they have learned. In school there are always three different kinds of students: One, those who were hard workers and who got good grades; two, those who were average and simply got through; and, three, those who were merely bidding their time waiting to get out! Jesus finds the same among His followers: Those who are committed, wanting to grow and blossom into what God is calling them to be and to do; those who are saved, but not sure how much of this they want to get involved; and, those who are just bidding their time. Just like those students in school, we know who is getting most out of it, we know who are going to make the biggest difference in the world as a result of their level of commitment.

The same principle applies to our work for Jesus. But there is a major difference, what happens in school is very temporary, what we do for Jesus lasts for eternity! The call of Jesus on our lives is not to simply become "belong-ers" but rather to become disciples, full-time learners, growing into His likeness, excited about the faith enough to share it so that we can reach out and win people for Christ!

V. To Send

The last purpose for believers we are going to look at is to send. If we are reaching out, winning people to Christ and growing as disciples, we as members of His body will be encouraging people to go out to do His work. As members of the Body of Jesus Christ, we leave our place of worship every Sunday morning with a benediction, with a blessing. However, best applied, it is a blessing over the work that we will do for Jesus until we meet again in that place! It is a blessing to go out into the world to take your faith with you, to share it, to reach out, to win, to be disciples of Jesus. The real work of a believer isn't what we do inside the four walls of the church building, it is what we do outside of them! Worship, Bible Study, Fellowship are all part of our preparation for sharing the life and love of God after we leave the fellowship of believers! As the Body of Jesus Christ, we also send people other places to carry the excitement we have for the work of God in our lives, and wanting to share that life with others. That was our focus in the last chapter in becoming a Person of Missions.

We hear reports from missionaries, the long-term ones and the short-term ones and we get excited for the work they are doing. But, do you know what, you must be a major part of that work when you help to send these missionaries off to share their joy and their love with others who need to hear it. You do it when you support missions every Sunday, you do it when you pray for the people working in the prisons, you do it when you give toward the work of people sharing in the inner-city missions, you do it when you contribute to the work in foreign lands. However, you also do it when you share what you've experienced on Sunday morning with your family and your friends and others that you meet. You do it in the myriad of other ways you reach out with the love of Jesus to the world around us.

VI. Conclusion

I would like to challenge each one of us to consider where we fit into all of this. Are we as individuals manifestations of His church, reaching out to those who are lost? Are we winning people to Jesus with our enthusiasm and joy for all that He means to us? Are we becoming disciples so that we can be more effective in our work for Him? Are we being sent forth to carry out the work Christ has called us to as His Church, as His Body in the world today? Are we living out the purpose that God intended for His followers? Are we living out the purpose that God intended for us?

Chapter 14
"Becoming an Acts 29 Believer:
A Person of Growth"

Ephesians 4:1-16

Unity in the Body of Christ

"[1]As a prisoner for the Lord, then, I urge you to live a life worthy of the calling you have received. [2]Be completely humble and gentle; be patient, bearing with one another in love. [3]Make every effort to keep the unity of the Spirit through the bond of peace. [4]There is one body and one Spirit—just as you were called to one hope when you were called—[5]one Lord, one faith, one baptism; [6]one God and Father of all, who is over all and through all and in all.

[7]But to each one of us grace has been given as Christ apportioned it. [8]This is why it says: "When he ascended on high, he led captives in his train and gave gifts to men." [9](What does "he ascended" mean except that he also descended to the lower, earthly regions? [10]He who descended is the very one who ascended higher than all the heavens, in order to fill the whole universe.) [11]It was he who gave some to be apostles, some to be prophets, some to be evangelists, and some to be pastors and teachers, [12]to prepare God's people for works of service, so that the body of Christ may be built up [13]until we all reach unity in the faith and in the knowledge of the Son of God and become mature, attaining to the whole measure of the fullness of Christ.

[14]Then we will no longer be infants, tossed back and forth by the waves, and blown here and there by every wind of teaching and by the

cunning and craftiness of men in their deceitful scheming. [15]Instead, speaking the truth in love, we will in all things grow up into him who is the Head, that is, Christ. [16]From him the whole body, joined and held together by every supporting ligament, grows and builds itself up in love, as each part does its work."

Acts 2: 37-47

"[37]When the people heard this, they were cut to the heart and said to Peter and the other apostles, "Brothers, what shall we do?"

[38]Peter replied, "Repent and be baptized, every one of you, in the name of Jesus Christ for the forgiveness of your sins. And you will receive the gift of the Holy Spirit. [39]The promise is for you and your children and for all who are far off—for all whom the Lord our God will call."

[40]With many other words he warned them; and he pleaded with them, "Save yourselves from this corrupt generation." [41]Those who accepted his message were baptized, and about three thousand were added to their number that day.

The Fellowship of the Believers

[42]They devoted themselves to the apostles' teaching and to the fellowship, to the breaking of bread and to prayer. [43]Everyone was filled with awe, and many wonders and miraculous signs were done by the apostles. [44]All the believers were together and had everything in common. [45]Selling their possessions and goods, they gave to anyone as he had need. [46]Every day they continued to meet together in the temple courts. They broke bread in their homes and ate together with glad and sincere hearts, [47]praising God and enjoying the favor of all the people. And the Lord added to their number daily those who were being saved."

I. Introduction

In the last few chapters we've been looking at what it takes to become an Acts 29 Believer, a believer modeled after that exciting First Century Church we read about in Acts. We've seen that being a Person of Prayer, A Person of Missions, and a Person that is pursuing the Purposes of God are all what brings us to moving in the direction God is wanting us to go. We have four more areas that we will be looking at in the next few chapters: Teaching, Worship, and Vision, and in this chapter we are going to look at Growth. Growth is a subject that is somewhat difficult to talk about in the Church because you always run the risk of looking to be self-serving, growing your own kingdom, advancing your own church. But when we talk of Growth as it relates to the work of Jesus Christ in the world, we are talking about Kingdom Growth, not individual church growth, we are talking about being part of the exciting work of growing His kingdom in our world!

Growth in the Church is always two-fold. There is Spiritual growth and then there is numerical growth. To a large degree, one always follows the other. All the Scripture that we read at the beginning of this chapter speaks of this concept, so let's first take a look at Spiritual Growth.

II. Spiritual Growth

What does it mean to grow Spiritually? To grow spiritually as a believer means that we are becoming more and more like Jesus everyday! It's really that simple, but it's hardly easy! This kind of growth doesn't happen by accident. It is something we must be mindful of doing every minute of every day. It's one of the reasons that our church wrote their Mission Statement the way that they did: **"To follow Jesus Christ by knowing, growing, and showing His love and joy in a genuine way every day!"** Growing is an essential element of that statement and doing it every day is critical to making it happen! It would be nice if it did happen by accident, that spiritual maturity and growth just happened by osmosis. But it never has been that way and it never will be that way!

Growth comes through a plan, as we allow God to come and move and direct our lives! It comes as a purposeful, willful act that we commit ourselves to carrying out every minute of every day. Trying to become more like Jesus is a very unnatural act, it runs counter to everything our human nature desires. In fact, the only thing that does come naturally to us as human beings is the desire to sin. And, like anything else in life worth doing, it takes effort, time, training, and desire. There is a wonderful parallel made for us by some professional athletes. One example would be Larry Bird, who was one of the greatest basketball players of all time. Larry Bird had a gift, but he grew in that gift only as he practiced countless hours toward improving himself, even when he was at the top of his game he still got up every morning and shot 500 baskets. He poured over the game plans, he memorized the other teams strengths and weaknesses, he went out on the court for hours every single day to practice. He was a natural at playing basketball, but he knew that unless he put the effort in, no matter what kind of natural talent he had, it wasn't enough. He once said that he knew that he had to be prepared for the other guy with similar gifts who had practiced just as hard!

Obviously I can't touch on every single thing that we can do to grow spiritually, that is not the focus of this work, but in the Scripture we read at the outset of the chapter, we find the keys! The first key is found in verse 1 of Ephesians 4: *"I urge you to live a life worthy of the calling you have received."* This is Paul's prayer for the people in Ephesus to grow into the people God intended them to be. He goes on to elaborate by declaring them to be bound together by love and the unity of the Spirit, growing so that they would no longer be infants in the faith. One of the key dangers of remaining infants in the Lord is that we can be so easily led astray from the truth. Beginning in verse 11, Paul goes on to say that God has given leadership gifts to the Church, he writes: *"It was he who gave some to be apostles, some to be prophets, some to be evangelists, and some to be pastors and teachers, to prepare God's people for works of service, so that the body of Christ may be built up until we all reach unity in the faith and in the knowledge of the Son of God and become mature, attaining to the whole measure of the fullness of Christ. Then we will no longer be infants, tossed back and forth by the waves, and blown here and there by every wind of teaching and by the cunning and craftiness of men in their deceitful scheming. Instead, speaking the truth in love, we will in all things grow up into him who is the Head, that is, Christ."*

Do you know what happens when we fail to yield to the structure that God has developed in the Church? Not following the leadership God has placed over us is the key to the destruction of much of modern Christianity. It represents nothing short of a rebellion against God. Not that we are to be blindly leading anyone, but following with discernment based on the Word of God and the leading of the Holy Spirit. Rebellion takes on a lot of faces, failure to attend Worship, lack of participation in the life of the church, failure to communicate with one another, just to name a few. God provided leadership for the church so that the church could grow and prosper! The key is to listen and move and grow within the church. That's exactly what was happening in the early church from the beginning. The people follow the leadership of the disciples, they listened to the teaching of Jesus Christ, and they obeyed the commandments of their God. The result was growth!

The second key is found in Acts 2:42: *"They devoted themselves to the apostles' teaching and to the fellowship, to the breaking of bread and to prayer."* We can't worship God if we don't know Him. We can't become like someone we don't know or don't know very well. Did you ever have someone you liked and admired so much you began to act and be like that person? Imitating another person is always dangerous, but imitating Jesus Christ is precisely what we are called to do. The only way to do that is to spend time with Him and get to know Him and then you can imitate Him. That's how we become more Christ-like, as we are around Him, knowing Him and imitating Him in our daily walk we become more like Him.

We do this through our prayer life, which is why a Prayer Meeting is so important and our daily private prayer time needs to be inviolate. We do this through Bible Study, in fact that is why Bible Study is so vitally important and why we all need to be studying the Word. We do this in our day-to-day living by asking the question, *"What would Jesus Do?"* Additionally, and most importantly, we have Someone who will lead us and direct us and allow us to experience the Presence of Jesus Christ every minute of every day and He is dwelling within our very hearts, His precious Holy Spirit! But once again, this is not something that comes naturally, we must be open to His moving in our lives, which we learn through living and growing in Christ as we desire to do so! And when we are growing spiritually, then we will also be growing numerically.

III. Numerical Growth

The more excited we are about what the Lord is doing in our lives, about our growing faith, about what's happening around us, the more we will want others to come and be a part of the exciting things that God is doing. I've been a member of various groups or organizations over the years that didn't really inspire me. I've felt like I needed to be there because I had joined the group, but there was no excitement and not much going on and I never invited or asked anyone else to come join me in that work. However, I've also been in groups where there's lots going on and I'm excited about and almost always in those cases, I couldn't wait to tell people about what was happening! This is what was happening in the early church here in Jerusalem that we read about in the passage at the beginning of the chapter and have been talking about for the past several chapters! Acts 2: 46-47 reads: *"Every day they continued to meet together in the temple courts. They broke bread in their homes and ate together with glad and sincere hearts, praising God and enjoying the favor of all the people. And the Lord added to their number daily those who were being saved."*

Now let me give you a clue. It wasn't God or Jesus, in the streets in the flesh, sharing the Good News, it wasn't the professional clergy, because there weren't any, it wasn't the Evangelism Committee (they didn't have one of those either), it wasn't good publicity or a big name singer. It was the people of God on the move, inviting others in the power of the Holy Spirit and souls were being saved! The question of the hour is: "Does this still work today?" Is the Holy Spirit still as active and alive today as He was 2000 years ago on the streets of Jerusalem? The answer is found in the Word: *"God is the same yesterday, today, and forever!"* His power is the same today as it was in those early days of the Church. His Spirit is as active today as it has ever been.

Look at the Church in Korea and what has happened there, literally hundreds of thousands of active and committed believers coming together daily to pray and worship and lead others to the Lord! Look at the Church in Africa and what's going on there.

I get a praise report twice a week from my friend Robert of all that God is doing in their midst in the rural areas of Uganda. Look at the Church in South America, God is growing that church faster than almost anywhere else on earth. Look at what is happening in the midst of terrible devastation and despair in Haiti and all that God is doing there, people are excited, filled with joy, overwhelmed with the power of the Spirit in their midst!

God is on the move, His Spirit is moving as never before in history. We as His followers are being called into obedience under His Lordship in ways that we have never seen before. It is an exciting time to be alive, an exciting time to be a follower of Jesus Christ, an exciting time to be a part of the Church, an exciting time to partner with Him in His work. Around the world more people are coming to Christ than ever before! Why not here? Wouldn't you want to be a part of something that exciting for the Kingdom of God?

IV. Conclusion

It starts with you! Are you growing? Are you excited about your faith? Are you inviting and sharing the Good News we have? Are you ready to be a part of the greatest movement of the Spirit of God in the history of mankind? Are you ready for what God is going to do right in your own backyard?

So here's a test and here's a challenge! A short term challenge, while the excitement is still ringing in your ears. Next Sunday, wherever you go to church, invite someone to go with you. Invite someone who is not already going to church somewhere, someone who does not know Jesus to join you in worship next week. There is no better time than now, no better way to put into practice being an Acts 29 Believer than to do what they did in the first century, to invite people to join them! This is a simple challenge to test your willingness to be a part of what God is doing in your midst, what God is doing in the world. Invite a guest to Worship next Sunday, it's what God would have you do every week and it's what God would have you do every day. Let's fill every seat in every one of your churches next Sunday!

Are you up to it? Are you ready for His challenge? Be an Acts 29 Believer right now!

Chapter 15
"Becoming an Acts 29 Believer: A Person with Pentecostal Power"

Acts 2: 1-13

The Holy Spirit Comes at Pentecost

"¹When the day of Pentecost came, they were all together in one place. ²Suddenly a sound like the blowing of a violent wind came from heaven and filled the whole house where they were sitting. ³They saw what seemed to be tongues of fire that separated and came to rest on each of them. ⁴All of them were filled with the Holy Spirit and began to speak in other tongues as the Spirit enabled them.

⁵Now there were staying in Jerusalem God-fearing Jews from every nation under heaven. ⁶When they heard this sound, a crowd came together in bewilderment, because each one heard them speaking in his own language. ⁷Utterly amazed, they asked: "Are not all these men who are speaking Galileans? ⁸Then how is it that each of us hears them in his own native language? ⁹Parthians, Medes and Elamites; residents of Mesopotamia, Judea and Cappadocia, Pontus and Asia, ¹⁰Phrygia and Pamphylia, Egypt and the parts of Libya near Cyrene; visitors from Rome ¹¹(both Jews and converts to Judaism); Cretans and Arabs-we hear them declaring the wonders of God in our own tongues!" ¹²Amazed and perplexed, they asked one another, "What does this mean?"

¹³Some, however, made fun of them and said, "They have had too much wine."

I. Introduction

John Wimber was a product of the Jesus movement in the 60's. He met Christ in a dramatic way, and began reading the New Testament, beginning with the Gospels and then on to the book of Acts. He was excited about what he was reading, but when he went to a church he was disillusioned. The polite and tidy service was over exactly on time. Wimber looked at some of the people around him and said: *"When are you gonna do the stuff?" "What stuff?"* they wanted to know. He said, *"You know, the stuff!"* He had been reading about the conversions, healings, deliverance and other miracles that took place in the early church recorded the book of Acts. But instead of signs and wonders, he saw no sign of anything that would make him wonder, except the deadness of the ritual he had just sat through.

I have been reading and rereading the book of Acts for years, but recently I began to see again that signs and wonders were not the exceptions, they were the norm for First Century believers. Healings and supernatural happenings were expected and occurred regularly. Now some explain this by saying we are living in a different dispensation and that the age of miracles is over. That it was for a specific time and place to authenticate the message of the apostles, but we no longer need that today. Really, does God really divide history up into neat little segments where He acts one way with one generation and a totally different way with another? If so, then God is not, "the same yesterday and today and forever." If He does respond differently at different times, then He is one kind of God at one point in history and an entirely different God at another.

Followers of Christ today need to discover once again that we have an unchanging God and an unchanging kingdom. We need once again to discover the power of Pentecost. We need to become Pentecostal believers, and I am not talking about a denomination or a movement, I'm talking about becoming an Acts 29 believer, one who looks a lot like an Acts 2 believer! We need to be filled with the Spirit. We need to be operating in the gifts of the Spirit. We need to see people's lives turned around. We need to see people healed physically, emotionally, relationally, socially and spiritually. We need to experience the unity of the Spirit as the early church did. We need to be living in genuine love for each other, and when we fail at that then we need to seek reconciliation. We need to have the fire fall and the people of God to rise up. It has been written, *"When God sends forth the Spirit amazing things happen: barriers are broken, communities are formed, opposites are reconciled, unity is established, disease is cured, addiction is broken, cities are renewed, races are reconciled, hope is established, people are blessed, and church happens."*

Today, I know that the Spirit of God is present, God is up to something! When the Spirit is moving and we are open to that movement then big things begin to happen! Discouraged folks cheer up, dishonest folks 'fess up, sour folks sweeten up, closed folk, open up, gossipers shut up, conflicted folks make up, sleeping folks wake up, lukewarm folks, fire up, dry bones shake up, and pew sitters stand up! But most of all, Christ the Savior of all the world is lifted up!

II. How Does That Happen

If that is going to happen in our lives certain conditions need to be met and certain perceptions need to be changed. We need a major paradigm shift. First of all, Pentecostal power comes when you realize: The Christian life is not about keeping rules, but about knowing Christ. Let me say that again, Pentecostal power comes when we realize that the Christian life is not about keeping the rules, it's about knowing Jesus!

As I was growing up in the church I heard a lot about being nice and how important it was to be a good person. We were told to be kind and to love everyone. If there was ever an opportunity to come to Christ, or an altar call in the church in which I grew up, I am unaware of it. In that church, everyone dressed their best and acted their best on Sunday. The service was predictable and formal. Don't get me wrong, the Bible was read and the preacher said all the right things I am sure. But there was no passion. I'm sure the words of the responsive readings were meaningful, but they seemed like they came from another time and place. Much of the service never connected with many of the people, or if it did, they were careful not to show it. Excitement was not exactly how you would have described the service in the church of my youth. No one ever gave a testimony.

Certainly, no one raised their hands or clapped during the music. And no one ever, ever said AMEN. As far as I knew, Christianity was about keeping the rules and being a good person. If you loved God you did it quietly and never spoke of it. The only disruption I can remember was the Sunday my sister and I started laughing in the middle of a woman's solo who was warbling so badly that it sounded like she was in pain. The twisting of our ears did not help much to squelch our giggles.

In churches all across the United States the "gospel" of being good is being preached. In some places it is translated as becoming politically active for social causes or at least becoming concerned.

In still other places, the measure of a person's Christianity is in how tolerant or inclusive they are in their acceptance of other people and ideas. But until we renew our commitment to preaching that Jesus Christ is The Way, The Truth and The Life, and that no one comes to the Father except through Him, we will not experience the presence of the Holy Spirit or know the zeal of those early believers. Until the people who call themselves the people of God renew their commitment to knowing Christ on a daily basis and living faithfully for Him, we will not experience the power of Pentecost. Until we live by repentance and faith, we will always be going through the motions of religion without knowing the person of Jesus Christ. As long as we think that Christianity is something that WE do, we are missing the point. It is not about what we do, it's about what God does in us.

Being a Christian is not doing the right thing or believing the right doctrines, it is knowing the right Person. It is not about being a member of the church or reciting creeds. It is not about baptism or communion, although those are important parts of our life together.

It is about surrendering my life, my body, my mind and my heart to Jesus Christ and asking Him to take up residence in me. It is about confessing my sin and turning from it. It is about banking everything I have and am on God and loving Him with my whole heart. The Christian faith is not a feeling. It is a reality. It is a real relationship with a real person—Jesus Christ. Christianity is about the most powerful and wonderful person in the universe who desires to know us intimately. And this experience is not tame, it's wild and it's powerful. In fact, if your experience is tame, then you better ask yourself if you are really following Him, because most likely, you're not! Paul said, *"I want to know Christ and the power of his resurrection"* (Philippians 3:10).

The second point I would like to make is that Pentecostal power comes when you realize that the Christian life is not just about salvation, but about transformation. There are many churches which are very different from the one in which I grew up. They faithfully preach about salvation and the necessity of new birth. In fact, that is what you hear almost every Sunday. The scripture changes, but the message is basically the same: "You need to be born again." And that's great as far as it goes. It is a necessary first step. But if our faith only consists of a single event where we repented of our sin and came to Christ, then it is an immature faith. What if a baby was born and we all celebrated the new life, but the baby never took in nourishment, was never nurtured, never grew, never developed. As wonderful as that baby's birth was, it would not survive. Pediatricians call it a "failure to thrive."

If you think that the Christian life is only about being born again, think again. It is not just about salvation, it is about transformation.

To hear some people talk, you would think that once we come to Christ we just wait around to go to heaven. We are just putting in time until Jesus comes. If that is the way we think, we will never experience Pentecostal power. We will never understand that Jesus Christ has come to establish His kingdom "on earth, as it is in heaven," and we are His agents through whom He works to make that happen. We are to grow in holiness, and be salt and light in a tasteless and dark world. We are to become transformed on a daily basis, through the spiritual disciplines and then become agents of transformation in the world. It is sort of like this: You can take ten gallons of gasoline and release a tremendous amount of power and energy by just dropping a lighted match into it. It makes a dramatic onetime impact. But there is another way to release the energy in that gasoline. Place it in the fuel tank of a new car, designed to get 30 miles to the gallon. The high tech engine will use that ten gallons of gasoline to take a person 300 miles or more. Explosions may be spectacular, but the sustained, controlled burn has staying power.

You don't want to be a flash in the pan, you want to make a difference in this world over time. You want to last for the long haul.

You don't want the Holy Spirit to just save you for heaven, you want Him to use His power to transform your life right now! You want Him to use you in this world for kingdom purposes. The kingdom is not far away in time and space, it is here and now. And to be a member of this kingdom, you need the power of the Holy Spirit operating in your life every day. The apostle John, in the book of Revelation, talks about all the things we have to go through in this world and says, "*This calls for patient endurance on the part of the saints who obey God's commandments and remain faithful to Jesus*" (Revelation 14:12). We must remember that patient endurance is very much a part of the obedience that leads to growth and power in the Church.

The third point I would like to make is that Pentecostal power comes when you overcome apathy with zeal. You can't try to be good and think that you are a Christian. You cannot just point to a past experience of being "born again" and say that you are a Christian. You have to grow. You have to want to be transformed into the image of

Christ and want to be made like Him. You can not be apathetic toward the things of God and His kingdom and experience Pentecostal power. A true transformation results in a transformation of the heart that loves God and desires to know Him better every day.

When we are delivered from the bondage of sin and ushered into the kingdom of God where there is freedom, we delight in the things of God. The more you know God, the more you will love Him and the more excited you will be about the His kingdom. The more you love Him, the more you will want others to know Him. The more you experience His presence and power, the more of it you want. This is the way to live. We have been forgiven. We have inherited eternal life. We have experienced eternal love. We are holding nothing back because we have discovered life. We have found the pearl of great price and it is worth more than everything else we have seen or possessed. Because of this we are excited about life and we are excited about the wonderful God we serve. We are willing to do whatever it takes to have more of him.

Chuck Colson reports that columnist Jonathan Rauch believes that America has made "a major civilizational advance" in recent years. Colson says, "Rauch, a longtime atheist, is thrilled about a phenomenon he calls 'apatheism,' which is apathetic theism. It's not that people don't believe in God anymore, Rauch writes in the Atlantic Monthly—the majority will still say they believe. On the whole, the people Rauch describes haven't been putting much thought or effort into their faith. They're looking for comfort and reassurance, not for a God who asks anything of them. Hence the rise of 'apatheism,' which Rauch defines as 'a disinclination to care all that much about one's own religion, and an even stronger disinclination to care about other people's.'" Colson goes on to talk about writer David Brooks who noticed a trend a few years ago and coined the term flexidoxy, which is a set of flexible beliefs. Flexidoxy describes the form of religion practiced by many educated young Americans as opposed to orthodoxy. Basically, it means that people have become flexible in their belief system and look at religion as a giant smorgasbord from which they can pick and choose the beliefs that most suit them. They become the center of their own faith and adapt it to what they see as important.

III. Conclusion

Many of you heard or read about 27-year-old Aaron Ralston who had his right arm pinned by an 800-pound boulder in a climbing accident. He had gone hiking in Bluejohn Canyon, near Utah's Canyonlands National Park. He was an experienced climber, for he had already climbed 49 other peaks in Colorado which were over 14,000 feet. He thought about what it would be like to die on the mountain and have his family find his body, or perhaps never know his fate. Ralston, a former engineer for Intel and an avid outdoorsman, thought about his options. After five days of being pinned, and having run out of food and water, he decided to apply a tourniquet and amputate his arm below the elbow with his pocket knife. He then rigged anchors and rappelled to the canyon floor with his one good arm. He walked downstream until he was spotted by a Utah Public Safety Helicopter. What the news did not say much about was that this Phi Beta Kappa graduate of Carnegie Mellon University credits his faith in God for ability to do what he had to do. He is a deeply committed Christian who often plays the piano in the home church in Denver. Because Aaron wanted to live, he was willing to cut away everything that was holding him back. It is that kind of commitment and zeal that will enable us to experience Pentecostal power.

When you are willing to cut away everything that is holding you back and walk out of the canyon of bondage, then the Holy Spirit will come to you in new ways and you will know a life that you did not know was possible. The Bible says, "*Therefore, since we are surrounded by such a huge crowd of witnesses to the life of faith, let us strip off every weight that slows us down, especially the sin that so easily hinders our progress. And let us run with endurance the race that God has set before us.*" (Hebrews 12:1)

The apostle Paul did this when he wrote, *"Brothers, I do not consider myself yet to have taken hold of it. But one thing I do: Forgetting what is behind and straining toward what is ahead I press on toward the goal to win the prize for which God has called me heavenward in Christ Jesus"* (Philippians 3:13-14).

How about you? Are you ready to forget all that is behind? Are you ready to strain toward what is ahead? Are you ready to run with endurance the race that has been set before us? Are you ready for some Pentecostal Power? Are you ready to be an Acts 29 Believer and experience the power the Acts 2 believers experienced? Are you ready?

Chapter 16
"Becoming an Acts 29 Believer: A Person of Worship"

Psalm 96: 1-13

"[1] Sing to the LORD a new song; sing to the LORD, all the earth.
[2] Sing to the LORD, praise his name; proclaim his salvation day after day.
[3] Declare his glory among the nations, his marvelous deeds among all peoples.
[4] For great is the LORD and most worthy of praise; he is to be feared above all gods.
[5] For all the gods of the nations are idols, but the LORD made the heavens.
[6] Splendor and majesty are before him; strength and glory are in his sanctuary.
[7] Ascribe to the LORD, O families of nations, ascribe to the LORD glory and strength.
[8] Ascribe to the LORD the glory due his name; bring an offering and come into his courts.
[9] Worship the LORD in the splendor of his [a] holiness; tremble before him, all the earth.
[10] Say among the nations, "The LORD reigns." The world is firmly established, it cannot be moved; he will judge the peoples with equity.
[11] Let the heavens rejoice, let the earth be glad; let the sea resound, and all that is in it;

¹² let the fields be jubilant, and everything in them. Then all the trees of the forest will sing for joy;
¹³ they will sing before the LORD, for he comes, he comes to judge the earth. He will judge the world in righteousness and the peoples in his truth."

I. Introduction
I've always liked hearing oxymorons, or self-contradicting phrases. The word itself comes from "oxus," which means sharp, and "moros," which means dull. Here are some of my favorites.
- Jumbo shrimp
- Freezer burn
- White chocolate
- Plastic silverware
- Airline food
- Sanitary landfill
- Truthful tabloids
- Professional wrestling

And, here's another self-contradictory phrase: boring worship. That reminds me of the little boy who asked his mother if she could remember the highest number she ever counted to. The mother didn't know so she asked him about his highest number. He answered, "5,372." The mother was puzzled and asked him why he stopped at that particular one. The boy responded, "Well, church was over."

We've been talking in the last few chapters about what it might take to become an exciting believer again, to become an Acts 29 believer, a believer that is modeled after and experiences the same results as the First Century followers of Christ. We've talked about being a Person of Prayer, a Person of Missions, a Person of Purpose, a Person of Pentecostal Power, and now, I want to talk about being a Person of Worship! In various surveys, when people are asked why they don't go to church, they often reply that church is just too boring. While I recognize that sometimes a church service can seem dull, especially to a non-Christian, I want to state emphatically that true worship is anything but boring. The very essence of what worship is does not allow us to be bored. When we come before the majestic God of the universe, Who has created everything and has done amazing things in our lives, we can't help but break out into adoration.

Psalm 95 tells us worship always should incorporate two elements: rejoicing and reverence. And, perhaps most importantly, worship must lead to a response. If we don't respond, we risk becoming hardened before Him.

II. The Heart of Worship

A close look at our text for this chapter, Psalm 96, reveals several key observations right off the bat. First, it's difficult to make divisions in this psalm because it's really a seamless garment of praise, woven together to catapult us into deeper exaltation. I'm hoping you got a taste of it when you read it earlier. Second, remember that this psalm follows the blunt indictment of the closing verses of Psalm 95. Since this whole section of Scripture, from Psalm 93-100, was sung as a majestic medley, we must be careful to not just pull out the parts and end up forsaking the whole. Third, this song of worship is based upon David's anthem of adoration as found in 1 Chronicles 16, when the Ark of the Covenant was brought to its resting place. In fact, if you compare the two songs, you will find a lot of repeated phrases. The context of Psalm 96, however, covers the period of time when the exiles returned from captivity. Fourth, this psalm is really a grand missionary hymn. The psalmist reminds the Israelites that the blessings of God were never intended for only one group of people. Fifth, the call to sing songs and break out into praise is given in the context of Christ's Second Coming and glorious reign. We sing not just because of the past and the present but because we know what's coming in the future. And before we go any further, let me ask and answer some basic questions.

Who should be worshipped? The Lord God is the answer! He is

mentioned by name or by pronoun in almost every stanza. What is worship? To worship means to "fall on your face or bow down" and is found more than 170 times in the Bible. We recognize our place before God and acknowledge His position before us.

How should we worship? With music (verse 1); with proclamation (verse 2); by giving Him glory (verse 8); by bringing an offering (verse 8); by coming into His courts (verse 8); by living holy lives (verse 9); and by witnessing for Him (verse 10).

Why should we worship? In verse 2, because God has saved us; in verse 4, because of His greatness and His fearsomeness; in verse 5 because of His power; in verse 6, because of His splendor, majesty, strength, and beauty; and in verse 13, because God is righteous and true and He is coming to judge.

Where are we to worship? We are to worship the Lord among the nations (verse 3); in His sanctuary (verse 6), and in His courts (verse 8).

When are we to worship? Verse 2 calls us to sing and proclaim His salvation day after day.

III. Four Imperatives of Worship

At the risk of breaking the flow of this holy hymn, I see four imperatives for us today, if we are to become a Person of Worship and truly experience the power and excitement of the early believers and oddly enough, they all begin with the letter "E":
• Exalt His Name (verses 1-2a)
• Extend His Kingdom (verses 2b-3)
• Express His Greatness (verses 4-9)
• Expect His Coming (verses 10-13)

IV. Exalt His Name

The first imperative is to Exalt His Name. We see this in verses 1-2a: *"Sing to the Lord a new song; sing to the Lord, all the earth. Sing to the Lord, praise His name."* We're called in this passage to sing to the Lord three different times. When something's repeated in triplicate it's done to get our attention. There has been singing and shouting from the beginning of time and there will be more singing at the end of the age, as the reading of Revelation clearly indicates! Since the world was created with a symphony of joyful praise and all creation will break into song when Jesus comes again, we're called to sing to the Lord in the meantime—as we wait for His appearing. Notice that we are to sing a "new song" to the Lord. This word can mean something that is brand new and can also mean, "delightful, precious and exquisite." When something is new, it is fresh. If all we sing is "Kumbaya," then chances are good that we're not growing and experiencing fresh insights from the Lord. While I love singing songs I already know, I really like it when a Worship Team in church teaches me a new one that remind me of the character and nature of our God! This expression "new song" occurs several times in the Book of Psalms indicating that fresh outbursts of rejoicing and reverence are important to God and helpful to us. Can you imagine what would happen if newscasts reported on last month's stories instead of what is happening today? It wouldn't be very interesting, would it? When I was little I had a paper route, and every day the delivery guy would bring me either too many or too few papers, never the exact right amount. I had an idea, I saved up the papers from the days when I had too many, and used them on the days when I didn't have enough. You can imagine the reaction that I got to that, nobody wants to read yesterday's news! I wonder if some of us are still reading "old news" in our spiritual lives. It's been so long since we've experienced anything fresh with the Lord that we're just living on the fumes of what we used to have in our relationship with Christ. Martin Luther has said, *"Christ is now as fresh unto me as if He had shed His blood but this very hour."* When we walk with Him daily and experience new ways of encountering Him, we can't help but break out into joyful praise and new songs. And that is precisely what this Psalm encourages us to do: Exalt the Lord in Worship!

V. Extend His Kingdom

The second imperative of worship is that we are to Extend His Kingdom. Take a look at verses 2 and 3: "*...proclaim His salvation day after day. Declare His glory among the nations, His marvelous deeds among all peoples.* " We actually are told how to extend His kingdom, we are to proclaim His salvation. We're also told when to do it, we are to proclaim His salvation day after day. And we're told where to do it, among the nations. Our message is the gospel, our method is to share the Good News daily and our mandate is to take it to all peoples. Our mandate as believers is to make sure this gospel message is not just shared with people we know, but that it goes out to "the nations" and "all peoples." In short, we are called to become "world Christians" who focus and pray for world evangelization. Jesus clarified this mandate when He said in Matthew 28:19: "*Therefore go and make disciples of all nations...* " I'm thrilled to be involved with a group of people who takes this mandate seriously as we partner with missionaries serving all over the globe from the New York metropolitan area to Central America to India to the Middle East, to Haiti and to many other places at home and around the globe. Representatives from every nation and tribe and village all over the earth will one day be in Heaven. Don't you want to have a part in helping them get there?

VI. Express His Greatness

As we Exalt His Name and look for ways to Extend His Kingdom, we will be drawn into the third worship imperative, we will want to Express His Greatness. Read out loud verses 4-9: "*For great is the Lord and most worthy of praise; He is to be feared above all gods. For all the gods of the nations are idols, but the Lord made the heavens. Splendor and majesty are before Him; strength and glory are in His sanctuary. Ascribe to the Lord, O families of nations, ascribe to the Lord glory and strength. Ascribe to the*

Lord the glory due His name; bring an offering and come into His courts.

Worship the Lord in the splendor of His holiness; tremble before Him, all the earth."

God is not just a tribal god, but is King over all the nations. He is most worthy of praise. While some people worship idols, only the Creator God is worthy of praise. Whether it's a professional athlete, an American idol or the President of the United States, we love to applaud the attributes of others. And yet, this psalm brings us back to what's most important—only God Himself is great and most worthy of praise. He is to be feared and honored above everyone and everything else. Verse 5 tells us that He has no rivals because He is the Creator. As such we should worship Him with all that we have.

In verse 6, four attributes are personified as if they were attendants surrounding the throne *"splendor and majesty are before Him; strength and glory are in his sanctuary."*

The psalmist has renewed urgency in proclaiming the Lord in verses 7-9. Three times in a row he challenges us to "ascribe," or give, to the Lord what is due His name. Because we recognize His greatness, majesty and strength, we will want to honor Him. It's interesting that even though "the nations" are called to worship the Lord, it is the "families" of the nations that are singled out to ascribe glory and strength to the Lord. God has ordained the family unit as a special and unique creation of His as parents. We must do all we can to make sure our families are honoring God through our times of family worship, interaction, and servanthood. We need to spend time in our families: reading the Word together, singing songs together, praying together; and, going to the throne room of grace together!

The last part of verse 8 gives us a practical way to do this. We are to make an offering to the Lord! I can think of at least three ways that we can bring an offering to the Lord today. First, Romans 12:1-2 tells us to offer our bodies to the Lord. When we surrender fully to Him, we will worship Him through the sacrificial offering of our lives.

Second, when we adore God with songs and hymns, the Word says that we are offering a sacrifice of praise. Third, we also worship God as we offer our financial resources to Him and His kingdom purposes. We bring our tithes and offerings because we have a deep need to express something important to God. Malachi 3 teaches that when we hold back in our giving, we end up robbing God and missing out on His blessings. When we surrender our lives to Him, when we offer a sacrifice of praise, and when we give financially, we are declaring that He is worthy. Verse 9 teaches that we worship the Lord in the splendor of His holiness through our offerings. When we tremble before Him, we will want to give all that we can to Him. Why? Because He deserves it.

VII. Expect His Coming

As we exalt His name, we eagerly will look for ways to extend His kingdom. This then motivates us to express His greatness. The final imperative is found in verses 10-13. Here we read of the reign of the Lord and His coming judgment. C.S. Lewis points out that this psalm looks upon divine judgment as an occasion for rejoicing. The word "judge" in verse 10 carries with it the idea that God sovereignly rules over the nations, and will judge everyone with fairness and equity. In verses 11-12 we see that the whole creation, when pondering God's rule, actually breaks out into joyful praise. The heavens will rejoice, the earth will be glad, the sea will resound, the fields and the flowers—will all be jubilant, and all the trees of the forest will sing for joy.

When Adam sinned, creation went out of kilter. When Christ returns, all of creation will be delivered from bondage. The last stanza of this hymn gives us great hope that Jesus is coming again. And when He does, He will judge the world in righteousness and the people in truth.

He will dispense justice, vindicate believers and will establish truth forever. His kingdom will have no end.

VIII. Conclusion

In the mean time, we are called to wait and worship. We also are called to tell others about the glorious gospel before it's too late. We also need to be ready ourselves so that we do not shrink away in shame when He suddenly appears. Jesus is coming again. You can be sure of that. And that has obvious implications on the way we sing, on the way we sow, and the way we serve. As we wrap up this chapter let me give you some practical action steps that you can take to become a people of Worship.

1. Read a Psalm every day.

If you start tomorrow morning with Psalm 1 and read a different Psalm every day, you will finish the Book of Psalms in 150 days. This alone will help increase your passion for worship. You might even want to read them out loud or sing them if you're able.

2. Listen to worship music every day.

I want to encourage you to incorporate praise songs and Christian music into your lifestyle. Some of you listen to other kinds of music or talk radio when you're in the car. Try to listen to a Christian station or play a tape or CD that draws you into worship.

3. Pray for 5 neighbors for 5 minutes for 5 days a week.

As we've discovered in this psalm, singing leads to sowing. When we praise Him we will want to proclaim Him. Begin praying for 5 of your neighbors on different nights of the week. On Mondays pray for one family, on Tuesdays pray for another. As you pray, look for opportunities to care and to share. This will help prepare your neighbors for the time when you are going to invite them to join you at church or at a special event where the Gospel will be preached.

4. Pray for missionaries on a regular basis.

I am certain that most of your churches currently have a list of missionary families you can be praying for. Maybe you could add missionaries to your family prayer times. Or, you could join a Prayer Meeting with some others to begin to pray for those who are serving the Lord on the Mission field.

5. Get ready for Jesus to come back.

If you don't have a relationship with Jesus yet, you need to ask Him to rescue you from your sins. If you're a believer, make sure you're walking with Him, and that there's nothing going on that would cause you to be embarrassed if He came back today.

I can think of one more oxymoron, and here it is: A Bored Believer. If you truly understand what being a believer is all about, it will be impossible to be bored. If you are exalting, extending, expressing, and expecting, you will be fired up and will experience the joy of what it means to partner with God in His kingdom work. And so, stop sitting, start singing, sowing and serving. I guarantee you that you will surely be the Acts 29 Believer you have been longing to be. And I guarantee that you will never be bored again.

Chapter 17
"Becoming an Acts 29 Believer:
A Person of Vision"

Proverbs 29:18

[18] "Where there is no revelation, the people cast off restraint; but blessed is he who keeps the law."

I. Introduction

We come to the end of our look at Becoming an Acts 29 Believer. I hope that it has been a study which will change your life. I hope that it has been a study which will change the life of your church, because it changed you as His church. It is my fervent prayer that you become an Acts 29 Believer, a believer modeled after those exciting followers of Jesus in the First Century Church, and I pray that you are well on your way toward accomplishing this goal! We have looked at becoming a Person of Prayer and hope that you are praying, you need to keep praying. We have looked what it means to be a Person of Missions and I pray you are turning toward missions in an increasingly positive way. We have looked at becoming a Person that seeks and honors God's purpose for your life. We have looked at becoming a Believer of Growth, both spiritually and numerically, and I will once again stress the critical nature of Bible Study and learning and growing in Him, and of sharing that knowledge with the world and being an infectious believer! We have looked at becoming a Person of Pentecostal Power and I believe that the Holy Spirit is falling afresh on our time more and more. We also have looked at becoming a Person of Worship, an excited, exalting, extending, expressing and expecting follower of the King of Kings!! And now we will conclude this survey by talking about what it takes to become a Person of Vision and about how critical that is for each one of us.

II. A Person of Vision

Where there is no vision the people will perish, the King James Version of the Scripture reminds us. Without a vision we are like a rock that has been skipped on the top of some lake somewhere that has no way of guiding itself, it simply goes where it goes. We are at the lake's mercy as to where we end up, how far we go, and when we turn or stop. We have no control over our own lives. Helen Keller was asked once "What would be worse than being born blind?" to which she replied "Having sight without a vision." What a profound statement by a girl who was unable to see, hear, or speak. She had no power over how she came into this world but she sure could help how she left this world. Let me be crystal clear, we can't help how we came into this world but we can help how we leave it. Without a vision the people perish.

The word vision means: sight, dream, revelation or enlightenment. The word perish means—to die or to expire. The question we must answer before we conclude our study is "Do you have a vision and if so what is that vision?" Close your eyes for me. Picture the terrible darkness that is all around you and think about that darkness as the world in which you live. Spend a moment surrounded by that darkness, experience the hopelessness of that darkness. Now, picture in your mind, a beautiful ray of light up ahead, poking through that darkness and beckoning you to come experience it! Picture the sounds of voices everywhere around you, milling about aimlessly in the darkness, lost and miserable just like you. Now you see that light, what's your inclination? Of course, go toward the light! Are you tempted to go alone or are you tempted to lead all those people you hear around you toward the light with you? I pray that it is your heart's desire to take as many people as possible with you toward that light! That's the vision I want you to have of what being an Acts 29 follower of Jesus Christ is all about!

III. What a Vision Is

Let me share with you what a vision is. First and foremost, a vision is the ability to see! It's really that simple! How is your vision? The sight I am talking about is beyond the natural. Listen to this passage from Hebrews 11: (vv24-27) *"By faith Moses, when he had grown up, refused to be known as the son of Pharaoh's daughter. He chose to be mistreated along with the people of God rather than to enjoy the pleasures of sin for a short time. He regarded disgrace for the sake of Christ as of greater value than the treasures of Egypt, because he was looking ahead to his reward. By faith he left Egypt, not fearing the king's anger; he persevered because **he saw him who is invisible!**"*

What we are talking about here is that Moses had a spiritual vision. He had never brought anyone else out of captivity. He had no clue what course was laid before him. He just knew that God was showing him a vision of something that was to come to pass in the future. As he stared into the burning bush the future and the past were revealed to him!

Remember what Helen Keller said when asked: *"What would be worse than being born blind?"* She replied *"Having sight without a vision."* Humanly speaking, Moses blew it when he refused to be called the son of Pharaoh's daughter. But Moses' vision enabled him to see into another world. Mark 5:36 reads as follows: *"Ignoring what they said, Jesus told the synagogue ruler, "Don't be afraid; just believe!"* What was Jesus saying? He was saying don't look with your physical eyes, rather look with your spiritual eyes. To see the unseen you have to ignore what people say and disregard what the world says (disregard = turn a blind eye to). Not only listen for just the audible voice of God, for God speaks in many ways. Don't be controlled by the logical, believe there is more to life than meets the eye. Whenever we go only on what we see with our physical eyes we run the risk of limiting what God has in mind for us. And unfortunately, we are all guilty of limiting God in that way. The Word tells us that we walk by faith not by sight. Our vision must be Spirit born, Spirit fed and Spirit led to accomplish what God wants accomplished!

How does someone get a vision? Take a good look at God! I saw a road sign not too long ago that said: "A good eye is one that looks to God." Once we understand how awesome God is, we will not hesitate to believe God for great things. Bruce Lee, one of the great marshal arts experts of all time, had a fighting style unlike any other because he developed it himself. The main part of his fighting style was to aim 6 inches beyond your target. What a concept that is for believers! Are we aiming at our target? No, in reality, most of the time we aim just about 6 inches short of our target, it's the best we can imagine! What if we could adopt this concept of aiming beyond?

What could we accomplish? Remember, a Vision is first of all, the ability to see! Are you seeing clearly? Do you look at the circumstance and not beyond?

IV. A Vision Includes a Faith to Believe

A Vision is the ability to see and a Vision includes a faith to believe! Listen to what Paul writes in Romans 4: (18-26) *"Against all hope, Abraham in hope believed and so became the father of many nations, just as it had been said to him, 'So shall your offspring be.' Without weakening in his faith, he faced the fact that his body was as good as dead...since he was about a hundred years old...and that Sarah's womb was also dead. Yet he did not waver through unbelief regarding the promise of God, but was strengthened in his faith and gave glory to God, being fully persuaded that God had power to do what He had promised. This is why 'it was credited to him as righteousness.' The words 'it was credited to him' were written not for him alone, but also for us, to whom God will credit righteousness...for us who believe in Him who raised Jesus our Lord from the dead. He was delivered over to death for our sins and was raised to life for our justification."*

It is my prayer that God would help you to have a faith in Him that is strong enough to believe. I like to think about the young father in Mark 9:24 *"Immediately the boy's father exclaimed, "I do believe; help me overcome my unbelief!"* We forget that God desires to and will help us do everything and that includes helps our faith in Him become stronger! How? Through His word. *"I can do all things through Christ who strengthens me."*

There are a lot of factors that influence our service for God which we have no control over, our background, our age, our giftedness. But there is one important factor that we do have control over, how much we choose to believe God. A 5th grade Sunday School class was asked to go home and count the stars in the sky in preparation for their next Sunday School lesson. They came back with various numbers. Some said 100, some said 1000, some said a million. Finally the teacher asked a little boy who had said nothing, "How many stars did you count?" He replied, "3." The teacher asked how did you only see 3? He said, "I guess we just have a small backyard." That's our problem when it comes to believing, we have a small backyard. Our faith needs to be strengthened and that happens through reading, hearing, and trusting in His Word. You don't need much faith. The Word reminds us that faith the size of a mustard seed can move mountains. But you've got to trust in the God you serve! A vision includes the faith to believe!

V. A Vision Includes a Courage to Do

A vision includes the ability to see and the faith to believe, and it also includes the courage to do! In other words faith includes action.

Courage is going forward in spite of fear. Was David afraid? Yes, but there was a cause. Our problem is that too often we want to live in our comfort zone. Look at what God asks most of our Bible Heroes to do. He takes matters out of their hands and asks them to put matters into His! Every Biblical hero listed in Hebrews 11 is there because they couldn't do something in their own strength! Every Biblical hero listed in Hebrews 11 is there because the situation in which they found themselves was impossible! But every Biblical hero listed in Hebrews 11 is there because they trusted the God who gave them the impossible assignment to do what He promised! They trusted God and then they went forward! We so often want to keep a tight grip on the things we can know that we can do, the things we can physically change or alter. We never want to reach beyond that limit of our own powers and abilities. But when God calls us into action and gives us an assignment, we have got to trust that He will give us everything that we need to accomplish that assignment. We have got to know that alone it is impossible, but together with God and the others He has chosen to join us in the task, all things are possible! We have got to let go of what "we" can achieve and grab hold of what God can achieve through us! That takes courage!

But look at what God asks most of our Biblical heroes to do. God ask them to attempt the impossible. What if these Biblical heroes did not want to move beyond their comfort zones? Noah would have said—*"Sorry God I don't do boats!"* Moses would have said—*"I don't like people, I'm staying with my sheep!"* David would have said—*"I don't do giants or kingdoms God I am just a lowly shepherd boy!"* Mary would have said—*"I don't do babies, that way anyway!"*

The biggest Goliath in most of our lives is our self. We wake up and look in the mirror everyday and see the same person we saw yesterday. We don't look beyond the reflection and see God's handiwork. Why don't we have more faith, more courage, more vision? It's not God's fault. In fact, if we could kick the person responsible for our doubts, we couldn't sit down for a week! God help us to be courageous in the task before us. A Vision includes a courage to do!

VI. Conclusion

Vision is the Ability to see what others can't. Vision is the Faith to believe what others will not. Vision is the Courage to do what others say can't be done. Vision is the Courage to do what our common sense tells us can't be done.

Christopher Columbus' diary at times seems to be very repetitive. Page after page simply says, *"This day we sailed on!"* What a great motto for a believer with vision. Anybody can start the race, but they don't give out the awards until you finish. Do you have a vision for your life? Do you have a vision for your children? Do you have a vision for His church? Do you have a vision for the lost?

Friend, I think you have the ability to see. Friend, I think you have the faith to believe. Friend, I think you have the courage to do what God wants you to do. Friend, I've concluded after writing these chapters that you do have what it takes to become an Acts 29 Believer! You can be a Person of Prayer! You can be a Person of Mission! You can be a Person of Purpose! You can be a Person of Growth! You can be a Person of Pentecostal Power! You can be a Person of Worship! And you can be a Person with Vision! You can be an Acts 29 Believer! So, let's get to work…

Epilogue

We've come a long way in our study of the Scripture and our look at what God is saying to you and to me as "the Church of Jesus Christ" in this day and age. We began our study by exploring what God says to each one of us as His followers through the words of His letters to the churches in the early chapters of Revelation.

It is my contention that we need to read every single word of these letters precisely as if they are written directly to you and me. The letters to the churches are indeed letters to churches, of that there is no doubt; but they are so much more than that. These letters are specific words of instruction to each of us as follower of Jesus Christ today and as such, the warnings for disregarding these words cannot be taken lightly. The instructions offered in these letters are not just given to us for the sake of being obedient, they are instructions given to us as followers of Christ for the advancement of His kingdom here on earth. God's plan all along was that His followers would be, with the aid of the Holy Spirit, the ones to advance His kingdom wherever we may be planted.

When Jesus offers the commendations to the churches of Asia Minor, He is offering us instruction on behavior that is pleasing to Him for His followers. When Jesus offers the condemnations to the churches of Asia Minor, He is offering us instruction on behavior that is abhorrent to Him if entered into by His disciples. When Jesus offers warnings for these behaviors, He is speaking directly to you and me and giving us the clear warning for our own behavior in our own time. When Jesus offers the promises to the churches for standing firm and remaining steadfast to the end, He is extending those promises to each one of us in the 21st century as we continue to be His church in our time.

When the Holy Spirit inspired Luke to write the history of the First Century Church it wasn't written just to record the events of those amazing days; it was also written as a clear instruction to the church throughout all of history. More specifically, the words of the Book of Acts are written as a clear instruction to you and me as disciples of Jesus Christ.

The final instruction that Jesus Christ gave to us before His ascension into heaven was this: *"Therefore go and make disciples of all nations, baptizing them in the name of the Father and of the Son and of the Holy Spirit, and teaching them to obey everything I have commanded you. And surely I am with you always, to the very end of the age."* Jesus gave us these instructions so that WE could continue to be the Church throughout the ages until He comes again.

It is my contention that we are still the church today and that all of His instruction applies directly to you and me as individuals and that we are responsible for responding to each instruction with glad and obedient hearts. It is my prayer that if nothing else comes from this work, that one thing would, that each reader of these pages would now begin to read the Book of Acts and the Letters to the Churches in Revelation as specific instructions to you personally, rather than nebulous instructions for your pastor to employ as he or she leads your church. Instead, remember that we are the church and that as such, you and I have the responsibility to answer the call.

Go, now, and make disciples of all nations and may you, as the Church of Jesus Christ, continue to grow and prosper until He comes again!